Walking in the Resurrection

Walking in the Resurrection

The Schleitheim Confession in Light of the Scriptures

"Baptism shall be given ... to all those who desire to
walk in the resurrection of Jesus Christ
and be buried with Him in death,
so that they might rise with Him."
Schleitheim Confession, Article I

"That I may know him, and the power of his resurrection,
and the fellowship of his sufferings, being made conform-
able unto his death; If by any means I might attain unto
the resurrection of the dead."
Philippians 3:10-11

By Andrew V. Ste. Marie

Sermon on the Mount Publishing
Manchester, MI

ISBN 978-1-68001-000-8

All Scripture quotations from the King James Bible. Italics in the quotations are not for emphasis, but were used by the KJV translators to denote words not in the Greek manuscripts added to complete the English sense.

For more excellent titles and other material by the same author, contact:

Sermon on the Mount Publishing
P.O. Box 246
Manchester, MI 48158
(734) 428-0488
the-witness@sbcglobal.net
www.kingdomreading.com

Our Mission
To obey the commands of Christ and to teach men to do so.

About the Cover
Nestled amid the hills and fields of northern Switzerland lies the town of Schleitheim. This is the place where the Schleitheim Confession was officially adopted by a group of Swiss Anabaptists in 1527. (Photograph by Hansueli Krapf; used under the Creative Commons Attribution-Share Alike 3.0 Unported license [http://creativecommons.org/licenses/by-sa/3.0/]).
Overlaid on the front cover are the title page of an early printing of the Schleitheim Confession and the title page of the Froschauer Bible – the favorite translation of the early Swiss Anabaptists.
On the back cover is an artist's impression of Michael Sattler.

First Printing—January 2014—1,200 copies

Dedication

To my blessed Lord and Savior, Jesus Christ,
Who took up the cross for me.
I will take up the cross and follow Him.

Acknowledgements

This project has been a team effort, requiring the help and input of many people. I am sincerely grateful to those who have helped in many ways. First and foremost, I thank and praise my Lord Jesus Christ, for Whom this book was written. If it were not for Him, none of us would be alive, nor would we be able to serve God acceptably. May His Name be praised.

I also thank my parents for the great amount of help they offered, especially in editing and offering helpful suggestions. Alan Troyer, Dean Taylor, and Matthew R. Ste. Marie also offered feedback and suggestions which improved this book. Mike Atnip gave valuable feedback regarding the book's text as well as designing the cover and the interior pages. Steve Miller gave encouraging comments, as did Peter Hoover, who also granted permission to use some of his translations of Anabaptist texts in the book. Jennifer Burdge copyedited the manuscript. My grandfather, Vincent H. Ste. Marie, gave a generous financial gift which helped to fund the printing of this book. Finally, MennoMedia, Plough Publishing, the Mennonite Historical Society, Ohio Amish Library, and the Lancaster Mennonite Historical Society all granted permission to use their translations of early Anabaptist texts.

Thanks to all who have had a part in this project. May the Lord richly reward you.

Introduction

The Schleitheim Confession of Faith, the first Anabaptist confession of faith, was completed and approved on February 24, 1527—nearly 500 years ago. Today, it is still honored and loved by many of the descendants of the early Swiss Anabaptists. But is a nearly 500-year old document still relevant to us today? Should it matter to us what a persecuted religious minority group believed and practiced in the 1500s? Should we seek a more exciting spirituality elsewhere, or return to the faith of the early Anabaptists?

This book seeks to examine the Schleitheim Confession with the light of the Scriptures, along with additional commentary from other early Anabaptist writings. The Schleitheim Confession, being a human document, is certainly not perfect; however, it is my conviction that the faith it outlines is the true, Biblical faith—the truth which shall endure to all generations. Therefore, even though it is admittedly old, it is not outdated. We need not seek something new and exciting to spice up our spiritual lives. We need to find what God has said and obey it. We need to trust Him fully and follow Christ, as the early Anabaptists sought to do.

Some of my readers claim the early Anabaptists as their spiritual forefathers. In this book, you will be able to read their own words about the faith which they lived and died for. Others of you may never have heard of the early Anabaptists, or you may have only heard negative things about the Anabaptist view of the Christian faith. I invite you to examine the Scriptures and the beliefs of the Anabaptists with an open mind. May the Spirit of God illuminate all of our understandings and lead us to accept "all truth" as He has revealed it.

It is not my intention to lift up the writings of the early Anabaptists to the level of Scripture. Scripture is inspired of God and is profitable to us (II Timothy 3:16), but we should also "mark them which walk so as ye have us for an ensample" (Philippians 3:17). Those who have gone before us in the faith have much to teach us, though as with all things, we must read and consider with discernment, searching the Scriptures to see what is true (Acts 17:11-12).

My prayer is that all who read this book would embrace the glorious Biblical principles discussed therein and be willing to take up the cross to follow Jesus.

To God be all the glory and praise!

~ Andrew V. Ste. Marie
June, 2013

Contents

Title page of an early printing of the Schleitheim Confession and other material related to Michael Sattler.

Translation:
"A Brotherly Agreement of Some Children of God Concerning Seven Articles. An open letter of Michael Sattler to a church of God, being a short yet true testimony, how he testified to his teachings with his blood at Rottenburg on the Neckar."

Chapter 1

The History of the Schleitheim Confession

The Schleitheim Confession came into being in the context of Reformation-era Europe. In 1517, the Reformation began with Martin Luther's challenge against the selling of papal indulgences. These were supposed to reduce time in Purgatory, an alleged "middle ground" place in the afterlife where heaven-bound people paid a temporal penalty for their sins. Luther's movement soon became the widespread Reformation, which completely shook the foundations of the medieval Roman Catholic Church.

The Reformation came to Switzerland in 1520 in the canton of Zürich, when Ulrich Zwingli, the new priest of the Grossmünster (the large Zürich city cathedral), pledged that he would preach nothing but the Gospel in his new position. The idea that one could preach only the Gospel and not church tradition was a radical one. Zwingli soon gathered around himself a circle of zealous young men who were also committed to following the Scriptures.

Unfortunately, under pressure from the Great Council (the governing body of the city of Zürich), Zwingli backed away from some of his earlier beliefs and allowed the Reformation to proceed at the pace which the city Council set. The young men who had been with Zwingli were very displeased by this development.

Under the leadership of Conrad Grebel, Felix Manz, and Jörg (George) Blaurock, a small group of Zwingli's former students eventually initiated believer's baptism amongst themselves (as opposed to the then-prevailing practice of infant baptism), thus creating (whether they realized it or not) the Swiss Brethren church or "Anabaptists" (meaning "re-baptizers"). This occurred on January 21, 1525.

The next years were busy for the three Anabaptist leaders. When they were not in jail or debating the Reformers, they traveled far and wide. They spent most of their time in Switzerland, preaching the Gospel of the kingdom and what God's Word said about baptism, the new birth, and how God designed churches and Christians to function. But trouble came to the Swiss Brethren. In the summer of 1526, Conrad Grebel, undoubtedly the young church's most skilled human leader, died of the plague. In 1527, Felix Manz was martyred by drowning and Jörg Blaurock was banished from Zürich. Later, he was banished from other Swiss cantons, and left Switzerland altogether. Furthermore, other men with other visions had accepted rebaptism and tried to spread their ideas. Balthasar Hubmaier, although a skilled defender of believer's baptism, was not nonresistant and seemed to want a state church. Others had spiritualist[1] tendencies. Without adequate, Scriptural leadership, the Anabaptist movement was threatened with imminent disintegration. In the midst of this trying moment in Swiss Brethren history, God raised up a man to do what was necessary to preserve a Scriptural church in Switzerland. That man was Michael Sattler.

---

1   The spiritualists rejected church forms such as baptism, the Lord's Supper, and a disciplined church body. Instead, they believed that an individual's spiritual relationship with God was supreme, with outward ceremonies being unnecessary.

Michael Sattler: Early Life and Conversion

Essentially nothing is known of Michael Sattler's early life. We know that he was a monk at the Benedictine monastery, St. Peter's of the Black Forest. He may even have been a prior there.[2] During the Peasant's War, the Black Forest peasants invaded the monastery because of their grievances against the abbot. After this event, Michael Sattler left the monastery and seems to have gone to Zürich, the very city where the Anabaptist movement was in full swing. Here he associated with the Anabaptists, but apparently did not join them right away. In November 1525, he was imprisoned but released when he swore an oath of loyalty to the government. He was not yet fully committed.

Sometime in late May 1526 or perhaps a bit later, Michael was living in the house of Hans Kuenzi, a former Anabaptist, learning the weaver's trade. He was probably baptized soon after this.

Michael Sattler evangelized in the Zürich area for a brief time. Sometime in 1526, he went to Strasbourg in southern Germany (now part of France).

Sattler's Stay in Strasbourg

It is not known precisely when Sattler arrived in Strasbourg. His purpose for being there seems to have been to intervene on behalf of some Anabaptist friends who were in prison there. In this role, he came into contact with the reformers of the city, Martin Bucer and Wolfgang Capito. Sattler carried on a dialog with the two for some time and became friends with both of them, especially Capito. Sattler also may have met Hans Denck, a spiritualist Anabaptist, and Ludwig

---

2   The prior held the second position of authority in the monastery, under the abbot.

Haetzer, a scholar who was later marginally involved with the Anabaptists. Here Sattler was exposed to various other ideas of reformation and church renewal in the form of state-church Protestantism of a slightly different stripe from Zwingli's version and the spiritualistic ideals of Hans Denck. Sattler conversed in a friendly manner with the Reformers, but he found them completely uninterested in an uncompromising rebuilding of the apostolic church. Bucer and Capito, when confronted with Sattler's arguments in favor of believer's baptism, nonresistance, separation from the world, and abstinence from the swearing of oaths, constantly replied that "love is the end of the law" (from I Timothy 1:5). They argued that from a standpoint of "love," believer's baptism should not be insisted upon since the "weak" may still prefer infant baptism. Michael Sattler was unsatisfied with allowing this one verse, taken out of context, to overturn all of the New Testament commands. He doubtless knew that Jesus Christ is *only* the author of eternal salvation to those who OBEY HIM (Hebrews 5:9).

Finding that he had reached an impasse, Sattler left Strasbourg in late 1526 or early 1527. He left behind a letter for Bucer and Capito, explaining his departure. He addressed them as his "beloved brothers in God Capito and Bucer," showing that he did (at least at that time) consider them brothers in the faith. He then went on to give, in 20 points, why he could not agree with their easy appeal to I Timothy 1:5 to explain everything away. In this letter, he wrote, "But they are the true Christians who practice in deed the teaching of Christ."

The parting between Sattler and the reformers was peaceful on every side. After Sattler's martyrdom, Capito wrote a letter to the Council of Horb, in which he said:

This Michael was known to us here in Strasbourg and did hold to some errors regarding the Word, which we sought faithfully to show him by Scripture. But since besides in addition to our faithful teaching and that of other preachers there may well be shortcomings among the people who claim to be Christian, a life found to be offensive, it was for this reason, if I understand, that he took so little to heart what we basically argued to clarify the truth. But he demonstrated at all times an excellent zeal for the honor of God and the church of Christ, which he desired to see righteous and honorable, free of vices, irreproachable, and to be by their righteous life a help to those who are without. This intention we never reprimanded but rather praised and encouraged. But the means he proposed and his articles we rejected, in all friendliness toward him as a fellow member in Christ. . . .Now we were not in agreement with him as he wished to make Christians righteous by their acceptance of articles and an outward commitment. This we thought to be the beginning of a new monasticism.[3]

After leaving Strasbourg, Sattler evangelized for a short time in the city of Lahr, and then departed for Schleitheim for the famous conference.

The Schleitheim Conference

Undoubtedly the Schleitheim conference is one of the most important events in Anabaptist history, and Michael Sattler played a pivotal role in the conference. Unfortunately, besides the articles which were adopted at it, little is known

---

3   John H. Yoder, editor, *The Legacy of Michael Sattler*, 1973, Herald Press, p. 87.

about the conference—attendance lists were not kept, records of debates and speeches given were not taken, and we do not even know for sure where the meeting was held. It is not known who called the conference or how it was called. Nevertheless, it is almost a certainty that Michael Sattler was a primary author of the Schleitheim articles. Other possible participants include George Blaurock, Wilhelm Reublin, Johannes Brötli, and Martin Ling.

The product of the conference was a confession treating seven articles: 1) baptism, 2) the ban, 3) the Lord's Supper, 4) separation from the world, 5) shepherds in the church, 6) the sword, and 7) the oath. There was apparently some disagreement regarding these points among the participants at the conference, but at the end, they had found perfect unity (or *vereinigt* in German). The articles were sent out in handwritten form with a cover letter and postscript, which were almost certainly the sole product of Michael Sattler's pen. The full title of the confession is *Brotherly Agreement of a Number of Children of God Concerning Seven Articles*.

In the cover letter, Sattler explained the necessity of the conference and the confession:

> A very great offense has been introduced by certain false brethren among us, so that some have turned aside from the faith, in the way they intend to practice and observe the freedom of the Spirit and of Christ. But such have missed the truth and to their condemnation are given over to the lasciviousness and self-indulgence of the flesh. They think faith and love may do and permit everything, and nothing will harm them nor condemn them, since they are believers.
>
> Observe, you who are God's members in Christ Jesus, that faith in the Heavenly Father through Jesus

Christ does not take such form. It does not produce and result in such things as these false brethren and sisters do and teach. Guard yourselves and
be warned of such people, for they do not serve
our Father, but their father, the devil.
But you are not that way. For they that are Christ's
have crucified the flesh with its passions and lusts.
You understand me well and [know] the brethren
whom we mean. Separate yourselves from them for
they are perverted. Petition the Lord that they may
have the knowledge which leads to repentance, and
[pray] for us that we may have constancy to persevere in the way which we have espoused, for the
honor of God and of Christ, His Son, Amen.[4]

These words have puzzled historians, particularly the iden-
tity of the "false brethren." Who were they? Some historians have suggested that the confession was directed—at
least partly—against Hans Denck, Balthasar Hubmaier, and
Ludwig Haetzer. However, the closest match for the specific teachings mentioned would be the Protestant Reformers
whom Sattler had known in Strasbourg, Martin Bucer and
Wolfgang Capito. Notice that the teachers under discussion
"think faith and love may do and permit everything," rem-
iniscent of the reformers' constant reference to I Timothy
1:5. So was the confession written against the reformers,
or against Anabaptists/Swiss Brethren influenced by the reformers? The latter idea is supported by the fact that Sattler said that the "false brethren" were "among us," that is,
among the Anabaptists. On the other hand, it is possible that
he was referring to the Reformers and intended "among us"
to refer more broadly to all of Christendom.

---

4   All Schleitheim quotes in this book from John C. Wenger, "The Schleitheim Confession of Faith," *Mennonite Quarterly Review* 19(4) (October
1945):243-253.

Although we will probably never know exactly who the Schleitheim Confession was directed against, it and its accompanying cover letter are an excellent apologetic against Protestantism and its tendencies. It clarifies the points where the Swiss Brethren differed from the Reformers and the Roman Catholics. It laid out a solid "constitution" for the Anabaptist churches.

The Schleitheim Confession was instantly popular among the Anabaptists. It circulated widely in handwritten form. By July 1527, a mere five months after the confession was adopted, Ulrich Zwingli wrote that "hardly any of your people exist who have not a copy of these well founded laws, as you call them."

Martyrdom of Michael Sattler

The Schleitheim Conference occurred on February 24, 1527. Sattler returned home after the conference and was arrested very shortly afterward and imprisoned with several others, men and women. Sattler knew his end was near and wrote a letter of farewell to the church at Horb, encouraging them to remain faithful to the Lord in spite of persecution.

Although some officials wanted to kill Sattler as quickly as possible without a trial (to avoid the risk of escape, as he was recognized as an important leader), the law required a trial and one was organized. Several delays occurred and it did not begin until mid-May. Michael Sattler was finally sentenced to death. The sentence, which read as follows, was carried out on May 20, 1527:

> In the matter of the prosecutor of the imperial majesty versus Michael Sattler, it has been found that Michael Sattler should be given into the hands of the hangman, who shall lead him into the square and cut off his tongue, then chain him to a wagon,

there tear his body twice with red hot tongs, and again when he is brought before the gate, five more times. When this is done to be burned to powder as a heretic.

Two days later, Sattler's wife Margaretha was drowned in the Neckar River. She had wished to be burned with her husband.

Events such as Michael Sattler's martyrdom may tempt us to question God's wisdom. Here was an outspoken soldier for the kingdom of God, killed at the very start of what promised to be a brilliant life of kingdom service. He had powerful writing skills and the Bible knowledge to stand up to Catholic and Protestant theological challenges and to encourage people to live out the faith in spite of spectacular odds. However, God used Michael's heroic martyrdom to spread Sattler's own Biblical writings even further: Several accounts of Sattler's death were written and published. These accounts found such an enormous popularity that the Austrian government which had sentenced Sattler considered writing a counter-booklet, but concluded that it would be of no use. The Schleitheim Confession was later bound and printed with Sattler's letter to the church at Horb and an account of his martyrdom. This collection, printed in a book known as the *Sammelband*, eventually included other Swiss Brethren tracts. Sattler's martyrdom was better "advertising" for his writings and the faith than anything else could have been! Furthermore, it was a tremendous authentication of the faith which Sattler had defended with his pen—even at the cost of blood and ashes, he could still defend it!

Zwingli versus Schleitheim

The Schleitheim Confession was an instant "bestseller" among the Swiss Brethren and was distributed in handwritten form among them for some time.

In April 1527, eight Swiss Brethren were imprisoned in the canton of Bern. Berthold Haller, a prominent Zwinglian reformer in Bern, held several discussions with them and found that he could not Scripturally refute their positions. The lodgings of the imprisoned Anabaptists were searched and a handwritten booklet copy of the Schleitheim Confession was discovered. The Council of Bern (the governing body) asked Haller to write a refutation of the Confession. Haller did not even attempt to do so; instead, he sent the copy to Zwingli and asked him to refute it.

In the meantime, in Zürich, copies of the Confession were piling up on Zwingli's desk. He had already received his first copy from the Zwinglian reformer Johannes Oecalampadius. Before long, he had four copies of the Confession. He undertook the task of refuting it in his final book against the Anabaptists, named *Elenchus* (*Refutation of the Tricks of the Anabaptists*).

Zwingli knew that he did not want to spread the beliefs of the Anabaptists by publishing the German text of the Schleitheim Confession. To circumvent this problem, he translated the text into Latin and wrote his book in Latin, for the educated clergy of Switzerland. Ironically, the first time the Schleitheim Confession was ever printed was by the Protestant Reformers!

The *Elenchus* was written in three parts. Part 2 deals with the Schleitheim Confession. Zwingli calls the Confession "the grounds of your superstition" and says that even though they have never been printed, "hardly any of your people exist who have not a copy of these well founded laws, as you call them." Zwingli goes on to accuse them: "Why, pray, do you not publish what are so divine and so salutary? But counsels evilly conceived fear the light, and are terrified at the judgment of learned and pious men. For this reason you do not publish the dogmas, articles, principles of your superstition." Of course, the Anabaptists were a persecuted minority group whose access to the printing press depended on finding a printer who was willing to risk his life to publish their writings. Zwingli was being unreasonable and intellectually dishonest.

Zwingli called the Anabaptists' beliefs outlined in the Confession "fanatical, foolish, bold, impudent," then added, "This is not too severe." He continued to smear the Anabaptists, saying that the second article on excommunication "is all so crude that it smells of nothing but a three days' theologian" (that is, someone who has been a theologian for only three days). He called nonresistance "a kind of womanish gentleness." The many names he called the Anabaptists in this book include "monsters of deceit," the "heretical church of the rebaptized," "stupid seducers," and "vain seducers of old women."

The Confession Printed

After Zwingli's *Elenchus* was published in July 1527 (just two months after Michael Sattler's martyrdom), the Swiss Brethren were able to print the Confession in German. The earliest dated copy was printed in 1533, and included the Confession, Sattler's letter to Horb, an account of Sattler's martyrdom, and a tract on divorce which was (quite doubtfully) attributed to Sattler. Another printing, lacking the divorce tract, was printed about the same time. It is not known whether it was older or newer than the 1533 edition because it is undated. The Confession was also reprinted sometime in the mid-1500s and again in 1686. Dutch translations were printed in 1560 and 1565. A French translation was also printed no later than 1544, although this edition has been lost. It is not known what other material was in the French version, except that it did include an account of Michael Sattler's martyrdom.

John Calvin versus Schleitheim

In 1544, John Calvin encountered the Schleitheim Confession. It was sent to him from friends in France (where Calvin was originally from) begging him to write a refutation. Calvin's French book was translated into English in 1549, when it was printed in London; thus, in another ironic twist, the first Schleitheim material to appear in English was in Calvin's book. In 1552, the book was translated into Latin as part of a collection of Calvin's writings.

Calvin's refutation was titled *A Short Instruction for to arme all good Christian people agaynst the pestiferous errours of the common secte of the Anabaptistes*. He began by saying that the Confession book was "unworthy to be spoken of, or to be made mention of," and saying that he could "occupy myself, as men think, in better things." He apologized for writing a refutation of "a thing so barren and trifling, as is this little book, which appeareth to be made by ignorant people." He said it "hath no need of resolution towards them that have learning and understanding. . .in that it is so unlearnedly & foolishly written." Nevertheless, he stated that the book had been sent to him "from far countries" by "many good faithful men," who asked him to refute it, "with testimony that it was very needful for the health of many souls, that I should take it in hand." So he attempted "to shew unto all faithful Christian men which be rude and unlearned, what and how dangerous a poison this doctrine of the Anabaptists is: and also arm them by the word of God against the same, to the end that they be not deceived."

While Calvin wrote in a much more restrained manner than Zwingli, he still called the Anabaptists a long list of names, including "ignorant people," "poor fantasticals," "poor beasts," "dull-heads," "mad bedlams," "brainless men," "hogs," "beasts," and "mad men." He falsely claimed that the Anabaptists believed that the Schleitheim Confession was "a revelation descended from heaven."

Calvin's work revealed that he had little actual knowledge of the Anabaptists. One amusing error was in his commentary on Article II, on excommunication, where he wrote:

> We deny not, but that the excommunication is a good and holy policy: and not only profitable: but also necessary in the church. Moreover, that which this ingrate [ungrateful] people do know of this matter, they learned of us [the Reformed]: and by their ignorance or presumption they have corrupted the doctrine, which we on our behalf do purely teach.

Calvin obviously did not realize that the Schleitheim Confession was written in 1527, when he himself was an 18-year-old Roman Catholic and the Reformed churches of which he became a part were (as a whole) against excommunication. Furthermore, even before 1527, the Anabaptists believed in excommunication. In 1524 (before the first baptisms had even taken place), Conrad Grebel wrote the following:

> Whoever will not repent and believe, but resists the Word and the moving of God, and so persists [in sin], after Christ and His Word and Rule have been preached to him, and he has been admonished in the company of the three witnesses and the congregation, such a man, we declare, on the basis of

God's Word, shall not be killed, but regarded as a
heathen and publican, and let alone.

This was written when Calvin was about 15 years old. Contrary to Calvin's assertion that the Anabaptists had stolen
and corrupted Biblical excommunication from the Reformers, the Reformers learned it from the Anabaptists!

Why the Confession is Still Important

Some may wonder why it is worthwhile to study an ancient
Swiss Brethren confession of faith, now almost 500 years
old. The Schleitheim Confession is significant in that it reveals what issues were of importance to those faithful Christians who went before us. It shows us how they interpreted
the Bible and applied it to their lives. It shows us what they
were willing to suffer and die for. It offers us an opportunity
to see how closely our lives align with theirs and ultimately,
with the Scriptures. Although the Schleitheim Confession is
not perfect, and in some places it may have benefitted from
better wording, the faith outlined in the Confession is Bible
truth which is relevant for all ages.

May you be blessed and may the Lord Jesus be glorified
as we proceed to examine the faith of our fathers!

Sources
1. John H. Yoder, ed., *The Legacy of Michael Sattler*, 1973, Herald
   Press
2. Ulrich Zwingli, *In Catabaptistarum Strophas Elenchus* [*A Refutation
   of the Tricks of the Catabaptists*], translation in Samuel Macauley
   Jackson, *Selected Works of Huldreich Zwingli*, 1901, University of
   Pennsylvania
3. John Calvin, *A Short Instruction for to arme all good Christian
   people agaynst the pestiferous errours of the common secte of the
   Anabaptistes*, 1549, John Daye
4. J. C. Wenger, *Conrad Grebel's Programmatic Letters of 1524*, 1970,
   Herald Press

5. C. Arnold Snyder, *The Life and Thought of Michael Sattler*, 1984, Herald Press

6. John Horsch, "An Inquiry Into the Truth of Accusations of Fanaticism and Crime Against the Early Swiss Brethren," *Mennonite Quarterly Review* 8(1) (January 1934):18-31; *MQR* 8(2) (April 1934):73-89

7. J. C. Wenger & C. Arnold Snyder, "Schleitheim Confession," www. gameo.org/encyclopedia/contents/S345ME.html (Accessed January 6, 2012)

8. Christian Neff, "Calvin, John (1509-1564)," www.gameo.org/encyclopedia/contents/C296.html (Accessed June 22, 2012)

9. John H. Yoder, "Zwingli, Ulrich (1484-1531)," www.gameo.org/ encyclopedia/contents/Z97.html (Accessed June 22, 2012)

10. John Horsch, *Mennonites in Europe*, 1955, Rod & Staff Publishers

11. William R. Estep, *The Anabaptist Story*, 1996, William B. Eerdmans Publishing Company

12. Andrew V. Ste. Marie, "Living for the Truth: The Life of Michael Sattler," *The Witness* 10(9) (September 2012):3-11

Chapter 2

The Cover Letter

May joy, peace and mercy from our Father through the atonement of the blood of Christ Jesus, together with the gifts of the Spirit—Who is sent from the Father to all believers for their strength and comfort and for their perseverance in all tribulation until the end, Amen—be to all those who love God, who are the children of light, and who are scattered everywhere as it has been ordained of God our Father, where they are with one mind assembled together in one God and Father of us all: Grace and peace of heart be with you all, Amen.

Beloved brethren and sisters in the Lord: First and supremely we are always concerned for your consolation and the assurance of your conscience (which was previously misled) so that you may not always remain foreigners to us and by right almost completely excluded, but that you may turn again to the true implanted members of Christ, who have been armed through patience and knowledge of themselves, and have therefore again been united with us in the strength of a godly Christian spirit and zeal for God.

It is also apparent with what cunning the devil has turned us aside, so that he might destroy and bring to an end the work of God which in mercy and grace has been partly begun in us. But Christ, the true Shepherd of our souls, Who has begun this in us, will certainly direct the same and teach [us] to His honor and our salvation, Amen.

Dear brethren and sisters, we who have been assembled in the Lord at Schleitheim on the Border, make known in points and articles to all who love God that as concerns us we are of one mind to abide in the Lord as God's obedient children, [His] sons and daughters, we who have been and shall be separated from the world in everything, [and] completely at peace. To God alone be praise and glory without the contradiction of any brethren. In this we have perceived the oneness of the Spirit of our Father and of our common Christ with us. For the Lord is the Lord of peace and not of quarreling, as Paul points out. That you may understand in what articles this has been formulated you should observe and note [the following].

A very great offense has been introduced by certain false brethren among us, so that some have turned aside from the faith, in the way they intend to practice and observe the freedom of the Spirit and of Christ. But such have missed the truth and to their condemnation are given over to the lasciviousness and self-indulgence of the flesh. They think faith and love may do and permit everything, and nothing will harm them nor condemn them, since they are believers.

Observe, you who are God's members in Christ Jesus, that faith in the Heavenly Father through Jesus Christ does not take such form. It does not produce and result in such things as these false brethren and sisters do and teach. Guard yourselves and be warned of such people, for they do not serve our Father, but their father, the devil.

But you are not that way. For they that are Christ's have crucified the flesh with its passions and lusts. You understand me well and [know] the brethren whom we mean. Separate yourselves from them for they are perverted. Petition the Lord that they may have the knowledge which leads to repentance, and [pray] for us that we may have constancy to persevere in the way which we have espoused, for the honor of God and of Christ, His Son, Amen.

The articles which we discussed and on which we were of one mind are these 1. Baptism; 2. The Ban [Excommunication]; 3. Breaking of Bread; 4. Separation from the Abomination; 5. Pastors in the Church; 6. The Sword; and 7. The Oath.

—Schleitheim Confession, Cover Letter

The cover letter of the Schleitheim Confession explains the purpose for which it was written: a "very great offense" had been introduced by "certain false brethren among us." This offense was that they thought "to practice and observe the freedom of the Spirit and of Christ." In so doing, they were "given over to the lasciviousness and self-indulgence of the flesh" and thought "that faith and love may do and permit everything, and nothing will harm them nor condemn them, since they are believers."

As explained in Chapter 1, this is probably referring (at least partially) to the ideas of the Protestant reformers Bucer and Capito—perhaps referring to their teachings coming into the Anabaptist brotherhood. Today, Anabaptists/kingdom Christians still face the challenge of Protestant/Evangelical theology. Of course, not everything that the Protestants/Evangelicals say is false. We must be discerning and go to the Scriptures to differentiate between truth and error.

The early Anabaptists had to face Protestant theology in their day. Now it is our turn. We must 1) respond to it Scripturally and in love, 2) guard against its influence in our own brotherhoods, and 3) seek to convince those in Protestant churches to accept the entire Gospel and to begin living in obedience to the commands of Christ and the Apostles. Finally, and most importantly, we must PRAY! We cannot neglect prayer when involved in spiritual warfare! Do we think we can win without imploring the aid of the Almighty Lord of Hosts? May such a thought be far from us.

Can a man live in sin and go to Heaven?

The argument between kingdom Christianity and Protestantism boils down to this one question: Can a man live his whole life in sin and then go to heaven, simply by "trusting in the righteousness of Christ" or "inviting Jesus into his heart" without ever repenting and turning from his sin? Popular Evangelicalism asserts that faith (which is, to many or most of them, little more than mental assent to a list of doctrines) is all that is necessary for salvation, and once a man has that faith, he can live however he pleases without ever losing his salvation. It teaches a "gospel" of "faith alone," asserting that the "good news" is that no works are required in salvation. Is this what the Bible teaches?

> Know ye not that the unrighteous shall not inherit the kingdom of God? Be not deceived: neither fornicators, nor idolaters, nor adulterers, nor effeminate, nor abusers of themselves with mankind [homosexuals], Nor thieves, nor covetous, nor drunkards, nor revilers, nor extortioners, shall inherit the kingdom of God. And such were some of you: but ye are washed, but ye are sanctified, but ye are justified in the name of the Lord Jesus, and by the Spirit of our God (I Corinthians 6:9-11).

This passage teaches clearly that the unrighteous will not inherit the kingdom of God. Notice also that Paul is careful to exhort the Corinthians to "be not deceived." Do not let anyone deceive you! The unrighteous will *not* inherit the kingdom of God. No matter how much he protests he is "saved," if a man continues in these sins he will not go to heaven! Notice what the Apostle says: "such **were** some of you." Some of the people he was talking to were, in their past lives, guilty of the very sins he had mentioned, "but ye are washed, ye are sanctified [set apart], but ye are justified [made righteous] in the name of the Lord Jesus, and by the Spirit of our God." The only hope for the unrighteous is in repentance and turning in faith to Jesus Christ to receive the new birth. After the new birth, they will not be wallowing in those same old sins again!

Paul again makes this point clear to the Galatians.

> Be not deceived; God is not mocked: for whatso-
> ever a man soweth, that shall he also reap. For he
> that soweth to his flesh shall of the flesh reap cor-
> ruption; but he that soweth to the Spirit shall of
> the Spirit reap life everlasting. And let us not be
> weary in well doing: for in due season we shall reap,
> if we faint not (Galatians 6:7-9).

Paul again wants to keep the Galatians (and us) from embracing wrong thinking in this area: "Be not deceived"! Do not let anyone trick you! "God is not mocked"! We cannot presume on God's grace to live a life of sin and expect to get to heaven in the end. The Law of Sowing and Reaping is a spiritual law which is valid for all eternity: If a man sows to his flesh, he will reap corruption of the flesh. If he sows to the Spirit, he will of the Spirit reap everlasting life. We cannot expect to get by while continuing in sin, presuming on the grace of God or counting on some far-off "later" when we say we will repent. That "later" may never come.

Can faith and love do anything they please?

The reformers Bucer and Capito answered Michael Sattler's plea for obedience to the Scriptures with constant recourse to I Timothy 1:5: "Now the end of the commandment is charity out of a pure heart." Their argument was basically that love is all God is looking for, so whether one receives believer's baptism, is nonresistant, refuses to swear oaths, etc. is beside the point as long as he has "love." They argued that if some commandment (such as believer's baptism) was controversial or hard for some professing Christians to accept, it should be set aside for the sake of "love," since of course we would not want to offend anyone!

Is this argument valid? The Scriptures do not support such an idea. Jesus Himself told us what love for Him will cause us to do.

> If ye love me, keep my commandments (John 14:15).
>
> He that hath my commandments, and keepeth them, he it is that loveth me: and he that loveth me shall be loved of my Father, and I will love him, and will manifest myself to him (John 14:21).
>
> Jesus answered and said unto him, If a man love me, he will keep my words: and my Father will love him, and we will come unto him, and make our abode with him. He that loveth me not keepeth not my sayings (John 14:23-24a).
>
> If ye keep my commandments, ye shall abide in my love; even as I have kept my Father's commandments, and abide in his love (John 15:10).

John the Apostle later confirmed that love to God will cause a man to keep God's commandments—not set them aside or ignore them at will.

He that saith, I know him, and keepeth not his commandments, is a liar, and the truth is not in him. But whoso keepeth his word, in him verily is the love of God perfected: hereby know we that we are in him (I John 2:4-5).

For this is the love of God, that we keep his commandments: and his commandments are not grievous (I John 5:3).

And this is love, that we walk after his commandments (II John 6a).

If a man loves God, that love will cause him to keep God's commandments—no matter what other people say.

The Gospel According to Jesus

Most people, in explaining the Gospel, start with Paul's epistles. In so doing, they have tended to ignore both much of what Paul said and nearly everything which Jesus said. What was the Gospel which Jesus preached? Was it the easy-believism, "faith alone" Gospel which is popular today?

Jesus' first recorded message was very simple:

Repent: for the kingdom of heaven is at hand (Matthew 4:17b).

This is the Gospel in just nine words: leave your sins behind and begin to live in the kingdom of God! It really is that simple! Everything else is details.

What kind of repentance was Jesus commanding? Was it simple sorrow for sins? To answer this question, let us take a look at the repentance preached by Jesus' forerunner, John the Baptist, and His Apostle to the Gentiles, Paul.

Bring forth therefore fruits meet [suitable] for repentance (Matthew 3:8).

Whereupon, O king Agrippa, I was not disobedient unto the heavenly vision: But shewed first

unto them of Damascus, and at Jerusalem, and
throughout all the coasts of Judaea, and *then* to the
Gentiles, that they should repent and turn to God,
and do works meet [suitable] for repentance (Acts
26:20).

Both John the Baptist and Paul the Apostle taught that repentance is accompanied by fruit or works suitable for repentance. Repentance from sin means a turning away from
and rejecting of sin—accompanied by faith in God and sorrow for past sin. The life lived after repentance has occurred
is marked by an absence of the besetting sin and a positive
doing of the righteous opposite of the sin! For instance, if a
man repents from hatred, he not only stops hating his enemies but begins to love them. If a man repents of covetousness, he not only stops coveting, but begins to be generous
to the poor. If a woman repents of immodest dress, she not
only stops dressing immodestly, but starts adorning her inner
person with good works.

In Matthew 7:21-24, Jesus gave some words which are all
but forgotten by popular Evangelicalism:

Not every one that saith unto me, Lord, Lord,
shall enter into the kingdom of heaven; but he that
doeth the will of my Father which is in heaven.
Many will say to me in that day, Lord, Lord, have
we not prophesied in thy name? and in thy name
have cast out devils? and in thy name done many
wonderful works? And then will I profess unto
them, I never knew you: depart from me, ye that
work iniquity. Therefore whosoever heareth these
sayings of mine, and doeth them, I will liken him
unto a wise man, which built his house upon a rock.

There is a lot of crying "Lord, Lord" in many churches today, but in most of them, there is not much doing the will

of God the Father. Jesus tells us that only those who do the will of His Father in heaven will enter the kingdom of heaven. In the Day of Judgment, Jesus will turn away those who have worked iniquity (or lawlessness) from entering heaven. Notice, Jesus does not rebuke them for having trusted in their good works or their own righteousness, nor for having a wrong theology of the Trinity, nor for failing to have "faith alone." He rebukes them for working iniquity. Jesus then concludes the Sermon on the Mount with the famous parable of the two foundations. How does one build on the solid rock? Jesus said it was the man who "heareth these sayings of mine, and doeth them" that built on the solid rock. In other words, we build on the solid rock by obeying the commands of Jesus. He is a wise man who lives out the Sermon on the Mount.

In Matthew 12:50, we find another too often forgotten teaching of Christ:

> For whosoever shall do the will of my Father which is in heaven, the same is my brother, and sister, and mother.

Only those who do God's will are Jesus' brethren and sisters.

Jesus also taught that His words would be the standard on Judgment Day:

> He that rejecteth me, and receiveth not my words, hath one that judgeth him: the word that I have spoken, the same shall judge him in the last day (John 12:48).

Examine your own life by Jesus' words and ask yourself, "Have I rejected Jesus' words?" If so, repent and change your life now, because you will be judged by His words.

Must Christians Today
Keep Jesus' Commandments?

Some professing Christians have devised an ingenious theory whereby Jesus' commandments are relegated to some past or future dispensation, and they have no relevance to our present day. Thus, they may be set aside and ignored – not obeyed.

Not only does this theory have no support in Scripture, it is explicitly repudiated by it.

> Though he were a Son, yet learned he obedience by the things which he suffered; And being made perfect, he became **the author of eternal salvation unto all them that obey him**; Called of God an high priest after the order of Melchisedec (Hebrews 5:8-9).

From this passage, we learn that not only is obedience to Jesus' commandments expected, such obedience is actually necessary for salvation—Jesus will only grant salvation to those who obey Him.

In I John 2:1-6, we read:

> My little children, these things write I unto you, that ye sin not. And if any man sin, we have an advocate with the Father, Jesus Christ the righteous: And he is the propitiation for our sins: and not for ours only, but also for *the sins of* the whole world. And hereby **we do know that we know him, if we keep his commandments. He that saith, I know him, and keepeth not his commandments, is a liar**, and the truth is not in him. But whoso keepeth his word, in him verily is the love of God perfected: hereby know we that we are in him. He that saith he abideth in him ought himself also so to walk, even as he walked.

This passage tells us that one test of whether we are truly children of God is whether or not we keep Jesus' commandments. If you are wondering whether you are truly born again, read Jesus' commandments and see if you are actively striving, and largely succeeding, in keeping them. A true Christian will be able to keep Jesus' commandments; not perfectly, nor 100% of the time, but the general record of his life will be that he keeps Jesus' commandments.

In I Timothy 6:2b-4a, 5b, Paul says:

> These things teach and exhort. If any man teach otherwise, and consent not to wholesome words, *even* **the words of our Lord Jesus Christ**, and to the doctrine which is according to godliness; He is proud, knowing nothing. . .from such withdraw thyself.

From this passage, we learn that anyone who refuses to submit to Jesus' commandments and teach them is to be rejected and avoided.

The Message of Romans: A Life Above Sin

Many people seem to think that all God had to say about salvation is contained in the book of Romans. Many tracts focus exclusively on Romans to teach salvation, using a "Roman's Road Map to Heaven" analogy. Unfortunately, not only do such efforts totally miss Jesus' all-important teachings on salvation, they also skip much of what is inconvenient in the book of Romans. They have missed one of the major themes of the book: The Christian life is a life lived in victory over sin. It is beyond the scope of this section to give a complete commentary on the book of Romans, but I will simply point out a few of the often-neglected portions of the book.

One such passage is Romans 2:6-10, which says that God

> will render to every man according to his deeds:
> To them who by patient continuance in well doing
> seek for glory and honour and immortality, eter-
> nal life: But unto them that are contentious, and
> do not obey the truth, but obey unrighteousness,
> indignation and wrath, Tribulation and anguish,
> upon every soul of man that doeth evil, of the Jew
> first, and also of the Gentile; But glory, honour,
> and peace, to every man that worketh good, to the
> Jew first, and also to the Gentile.

This is very different from what Martin Luther and his followers say about what the book of Romans teaches.

Moving on to Romans 5:17 & 19, we find this startling
and exciting truth:

> For if by one man's offence death reigned by one;
> much more they which receive abundance of grace
> and of the gift of righteousness shall reign in life
> by one, Jesus Christ. . . .For as by one man's disobe-
> dience many were made sinners, so by the obedi-
> ence of one shall many be made righteous.

The grace of God given to repentant sinners makes the newly regenerated person "reign in life" over his old sin which
used to reign. Secondly, by the obedience of Jesus we are
made righteous—not just "declared righteous," but actually
transformed into righteous, holy people. These verses have
also been neglected by "Romans Road Maps."

In Romans 6, we learn about being dead to sin and alive
to righteousness:

> For if we have been planted together in the like-
> ness of his death, we shall be also *in the likeness* of
> *his* resurrection: Knowing this, that our old man is
> crucified with *him*, that the body of sin might be
> destroyed, that henceforth we should not serve sin.

> For he that is dead is freed from sin. . . .Let not sin
> therefore reign in your mortal body, that ye should
> obey it in the lusts thereof. Neither yield ye your
> members as instruments of unrighteousness unto
> sin: but yield yourselves unto God, as those that
> are alive from the dead, and your members *as* in-
> struments of righteousness unto God. For sin shall
> not have dominion over you: for ye are not under
> the law, but under grace (Romans 6:5-7, 12-14).

The majority of Romans 6 is composed of the type of admonition and reasoning quoted above. We are dead to sin so
that we can be alive unto righteousness. This means that we
no longer live in sin, but live in righteousness in practical
ways, every day. Notice that the passage quoted ends with
the phrase "ye are not under the law, but under grace." This
little phrase is quoted by many to justify their lawlessness,
but taken in context, it is a beautiful statement showing the
necessity of and ability to live holy lives!

What is Faith?

A foundational and important question is "what is faith?" Is
it mere mental assent? In other words, if I merely believe in
my head certain facts about God or Jesus, does that mean I
have true faith and am on the way to heaven? Paul the Apostle is quite clear about what kind of faith God is looking for:

> For in Jesus Christ neither circumcision availeth
> any thing, nor uncircumcision; but faith which
> worketh by love (Galatians 5:6).

It is "faith which worketh by love" which God wants—not
mere mental assent. This faith is active—it does not sit still.
Motivated by love, this faith does good for its fellow-men.

Menno Simons wrote:

> True evangelical faith is of such a nature that it
> cannot lie dormant, but manifests itself in all righ-
> teousness and works of love; it dies unto the flesh
> and blood; it destroys all forbidden lusts and de-
> sires; it seeks and serves and fears God; it clothes
> the naked; it feeds the hungry; it comforts the sor-
> rowful; it shelters the destitute; it aids and consoles
> the sad; it returns good for evil; it serves those that
> harm it; it prays for those that persecute it; teaches,
> admonishes, and reproves with the Word of the
> Lord; it seeks that which is lost; it binds up that
> which is wounded; it heals that which is diseased
> and it saves that which is sound; it has become all
> things to all men.[5]

What is Grace?

The doctrine of God's grace is one of the most beautiful
New Testament doctrines, but most people miss it entirely
because of an over-simplification of grace. Most Evangeli-
cals see grace only in terms of God's forgiveness of man's
sin, which is certainly a part of grace—but God's grace does
so much more than this! A good, brief definition of grace is
"God's power working in man." Read Romans 5:12-21 to
learn about the enormous victory over sin possible through
God's grace, and hopefully you will agree that God's grace
has been very underestimated by many Christians. You will
also see that grace truly is "God's power working in man."

---

5   Menno Simons (Dutch Mennonite), *Why I Do Not Cease Teaching and
Writing*, 1539; translation from J. C. Wenger, editor, *The Complete Writings of
Menno Simons*, Herald Press, 1984, p. 307.

What Does the New Birth Do to Me?

This is the core of many theological debates between kingdom Christianity and Protestantism/Evangelicalism. When a person becomes a Christian, what happens? The early Anabaptists answered that a new Christian was completely re-made from the inside out—as says the Bible. Today, many people answer simply that man's sins are forgiven. Although it is true that God does forgive a man's sins when he experiences the new birth, the new birth is much more than that! It is a radical transformation which makes him into a completely new man. The old man desired sin; the new man desires holiness. The old man was covetous; the new man is giving. The old man was selfish; the new man is concerned about others. The old man was hating and grudge-filled; the new man loves even his enemies. Many such comparisons could be made. The new birth truly begins a whole new life!

> Therefore if any man *be* in Christ, *he is* a new creature: old things are passed away; behold, all things are become new (II Corinthians 5:17).
>
> That ye put off concerning the former conversation [manner of living] the old man, which is corrupt according to the deceitful lusts [desires]; And be renewed in the spirit of your mind; And that ye put on the new man, which after God is created in righteousness and true holiness (Ephesians 4:22-24).

But the heart is all that matters!

This objection to holy living has been battled by sincere Christians for centuries. The early Anabaptists encountered it from the spiritualists, who claimed that literal water baptism and living in an organized church life with fellow-believers was unnecessary. They said that a man could just worship God in the heart while outwardly conforming to the practices of the state church. The early Anabaptists confronted such erroneous teaching head-on. Pilgram Marpeck, Dirk Phillips, and others wrote against it.

Today, and for many decades (at least since after the Civil War), similar statements have been heard from inside the churches of kingdom Christians. Usually, this objection has been heard arguing against nonconformity in dress. John M. Brenneman, an "Old" Mennonite bishop from Allen County, Ohio, refuted this argument well in the 1860s:

> Many, with all their pomp and decorations, still console themselves by saying, it does not matter so much about the externals, if only the heart is right. It is very true indeed that a good heart is the essential qualification in the true Christian character; but a good heart, beyond doubt, is also humble, and consequently can not exhibit any pride; for "a good man, out of the good treasure of the heart, bringeth forth good things."[6]

If it is true that the heart is all that matters, why does not the Bible say so? It is true that the Bible gives great stress to having a right heart, and a true Christian should be very concerned about keeping his heart right and pure. But the fact that the heart is not the only thing which matters in the Christian life is proven by the fact that Jesus and the Apostles gave many commandments about our outer life! If the heart is really all that matters, why would Jesus and the Apostles waste their precious time to give (and the space in the Bible to record) commandments about our outer life?

---

6   John M. Brenneman, *Pride and Humility*, originally published 1867, republished 2012, Sermon on the Mount Publishing & Primitive Christianity Publishers, p. 6.

Summary

The early Anabaptists in Michael Sattler's day confronted the evil world and proclaimed the Lord's word, saying "You must be holy!" They pointed out several specific areas where holiness was necessary in everyday life—and they demonstrated holy living. To them, true discipleship was not strictly a matter of what we believe in our heads, but was *following Christ* (*nachfolge Christi*) in practical ways in everyday life. Jesus continually called men to follow Him (Matthew 4:19; 8:22; 9:9; 10:38; 16:24; 19:21; 19:28; Mark 2:14; 8:34; 10:21; Luke 5:27; 9:23, 59; 18:22; John 1:43; 8:12; 10:4-5, 27; 12:26; 21:19, 22), and the Apostles repeated the call (I Corinthians 11:1; Ephesians 5:1; I Thessalonians 1:6; I Peter 2:21; I John 2:6; Revelation 14:4).

Hans Schlaffer wrote:

> To sum up, a Christian is a follower of Christ. That cannot be changed even if the whole world should end in ruins, which it will certainly do (and I believe soon).[7]

Menno Simons wrote:

> Whosoever boasts that he is a Christian, the same must walk as Christ walked. If any man have not the Spirit of Christ, he is none of His. Whosoever transgresseth and abideth not in the doctrine of Christ, hath not God. II John 1:9. He that committeth sin is of the devil. I John 3:8. Here neither baptism, Lord's Supper, confession, nor absolution will avail anything. These and other Scriptures stand immovable and judge all those who live outside the Spirit and Word of Christ and who mind earthly

---

7   Hans Schlaffer (?Stäbler Anabaptist), *Brief Instruction*, 1527-1528; translation from Walter Klaassen, *Anabaptism in Outline*, Herald Press, 1981, p. 91.

and carnal things. They shall never be overthrown, perverted, nor weakened by angel or devil.[8]

Wolfgang Brandhuber wrote:

> The one who fears God sees the true light and evaluates in it all his thoughts, his words, and his works. That true light is Christ, whose life is the will of God. In actual humanity Christ Jesus showed us what we should do, so that no one may have an excuse on the last day. Our thoughts on the inside and our deeds on the outside—all our life is to become a picture of Christ who said: "I and the Father are one."[9]

Today, it is our turn. Are we going to face the tremendously evil world and the mass of apostate Christendom with the Anabaptists' cry, "You must be holy!" or will we turn from the battle and, coward-like, join the opposition through conformity to it?

Jesus has promised that His church will triumph (Matthew 16:18). The question for us is: Will we be part of the triumph with Him?

"And let us consider one another to provoke unto love and to good works."

(Hebrews 10:24)

---

8   Menno Simons (Dutch Mennonite), *Foundation of Christian Doctrine*, 1539; translation from J. C. Wenger, editor, *The Complete Writings of Menno Simons*, Herald Press, 1984, p. 225.

9   Wolfgang Brandhuber, *An Epistle to God's Community at Rottenburg on the Inn*, 1529; translation from Peter Hoover, *Secret of the Strength*, 2008, Elmendorf Books, p. 37.

Epilogue

A Lesson from Sattler's Encounter with the Reformers

In a letter written soon after Michael Sattler's martyrdom, Wolfgang Capito, a Protestant reformer in Strasbourg and friend of Michael Sattler, wrote the following in a letter to the Council of Horb:

> This Michael was known to us here in Strasbourg and did hold to some errors regarding the Word, which we sought faithfully to show him by Scripture. . . .But he demonstrated at all times an excellent zeal for the honor of God and the church of Christ, which he desired to see righteous and honorable, free of vices, irreproachable, and to be by their righteous life a help to those who are without. This intention we never reprimanded but rather praised and encouraged. But the means he proposed and his articles we rejected, in all friendliness toward him as a fellow member in Christ. . . .Now we were not in agreement with him as he wished to make Christians righteous by their acceptance of articles and an outward commitment. This we thought to be the beginning of a new monasticism. We desired rather to help the believing life to progress by contemplation of the mercies of God, as Moses bases his exhortations to good works, on the reminder of divine favors and of the fatherly disciplining of the people by God (Deut. 8); which is the order of salvation.[10]

The reformers wanted to motivate good works and holy living by saying that these are the result of gratitude to God for

---

10   John H. Yoder, editor, *The Legacy of Michael Sattler*, 1973, Herald Press, pp. 87-88.

His work. Michael Sattler wanted to motivate good works and holy living by saying that they were necessary for salvation. Which side was closer to Scripture?

I will only quote one passage here, but I encourage each reader to thoroughly study the issue in Scripture. Why must Christians live holy lives? Why must they do good works? Hebrews 5:8-9 says:

> Though he were a Son, yet learned he obedience
> by the things which he suffered; And being made
> perfect, he became the author of eternal salvation
> unto all them that obey him. . .

Jesus Christ is the author (or causer) of eternal salvation to only one type of people in the entire world—those who obey Him. Are good works necessary for salvation? Yes, according to the Scriptures they are. Although contemplating the mercies of God may be a good motivation to good works and holy living, that is not why these are necessary. We would do well to stay with Michael Sattler's concept of obedience rather than the reformers' concept of obedience.

Chapter 3

Baptism

First. Observe concerning baptism: Baptism shall be given to all those who have learned repentance and amendment of life, and who believe truly that their sins are taken away by Christ, and to all those who walk in the resurrection of Jesus Christ, and wish to be buried with Him in death, so that they may be resurrected with Him, and to all those who with this significance request it [baptism] of us and demand it for themselves. This excludes all infant baptism, the highest and chief abomination of the pope. In this you have the foundation and testimony of the apostles. Mt. 28, Mk. 16, Acts 2, 8, 16, 19. This we wish to hold simply, yet firmly and with assurance.
—*Schleitheim Confession, Article I*

aptism was one of the most important issues in the struggle between the Anabaptists and the state churches (both Catholic and Protestant). The state churches practiced pedobaptism (the baptism of infants) while the Anabaptists rejected this and re-baptized those believers who had been baptized as infants. However, it would be a mistake to suppose that the Anabaptists were simply *against* infant baptism. They were *for* believer's baptism, which is *why* they were against infant baptism. Baptism is a solemn ordinance reserved for believers—it is not a rite of passage nor is it to be given simply because the person receiving baptism desires marriage.

Defense of Believer's Baptism

When we discuss the topic of believer's baptism, we are basically asking the question "who is ready for baptism?" Let us turn to the Scriptures, our infallible guide, to answer this question.

Let us first examine the baptism of John:

> In those days came John the Baptist, preaching in the wilderness of Judaea. . . .Then went out to him Jerusalem, and all Judaea, and all the region round about Jordan, And were baptized of him in Jordan, confessing their sins. . .he said unto them. . . .I indeed baptize you with water unto repentance (Matthew 3:1, 5-6, 7b, 11a).

What were the conditions of being baptized by John the Baptist? Notice—it was a baptism of repentance (verse 11). John admonished the Pharisees and Sadducees to bring forth fruits suitable for repentance (verse 8). Repentance is a change of mind about sin which is accompanied by a change of life. Those who forsake sin and walk in the power of the Holy Ghost have repented and are ready for baptism.

Secondly, we notice that those who were baptized by John confessed their sins. The New Testament sheds important light on confession, while leaving room for specific applications by individuals in their own situations. Who should I confess to? What must I confess? What about restitution? I would encourage you, if you desire baptism or are evaluating the validity of your prior baptism, to read and prayerfully consider Acts 19:18-20 and James 5:16 regarding confession of sins and ask if you are now (or were then) Biblically qualified for baptism.

The next passage about baptism which we will examine is Jesus' instructions in the Great Commission, found in Matthew 28:19-20 and Mark 16:16.

> Go ye therefore, and teach all nations, baptizing
> them in the name of the Father, and of the Son,
> and of the Holy Ghost: Teaching them to observe
> all things whatsoever I have commanded you: and,
> lo, I am with you always, *even* unto the end of the
> world. Amen.
> He that believeth and is baptized shall be saved;
> but he that believeth not shall be damned.

Notice in these passages who it is to whom Jesus gave
the authority to baptize: His disciples. Only those who are
following after Christ have the authority to baptize. If you
desire baptism, please be sure that the person who baptizes
you is a disciple, a follower, of the Lord Jesus.

> Beware of false prophets, which come to you in
> sheep's clothing, but inwardly they are ravening
> wolves. Ye shall know them by their fruits. Do men
> gather grapes of thorns, or figs of thistles? Even
> so every good tree bringeth forth good fruit; but a
> corrupt tree bringeth forth evil fruit. A good tree
> cannot bring forth evil fruit, neither *can* a corrupt
> tree bring forth good fruit. Every tree that bringeth
> not forth good fruit is hewn down, and cast into
> the fire. Wherefore by their fruits ye shall know
> them (Matthew 7:15-20).

Now we come to the instructions and practices of the
Apostles in regard to baptism. We find that on Pentecost,
Peter required the same of those desiring baptism as John the
Baptist had—repentance.

> Then Peter said unto them, Repent, and be bap-
> tized every one of you in the name of Jesus Christ
> for the remission of sins, and ye shall receive the
> gift of the Holy Ghost (Acts 2:38).

Again, have you repented? Did you repent—turn from your sins—before you were baptized?

Reading on in the same passage, we discover who was baptized that day:

> Then they that gladly received his word were baptized: and the same day there were added *unto them* about three thousand souls (Acts 2:41).

It was "they that gladly received [Peter's] word" that were baptized that day. Have you, or did you before your baptism, truly receive the Word of God in faith and believe the Gospel?

There are many other examples in Acts of the converts of the Apostles believing before receiving baptism. One of the clearest is Philip and the Ethiopian eunuch.

> And as they went on *their* way, they came unto a certain water: and the eunuch said, See, *here is* water; what doth hinder me to be baptized? And Philip said, If thou believest with all thine heart, thou mayest. And he answered and said, I believe that Jesus Christ is the Son of God. And he commanded the chariot to stand still: and they went down both into the water, both Philip and the eunuch; and he baptized him (Acts 8:36-38).

For other examples, see Acts 8:12, 16:14-15, and 18:8.

Another passage which gives us more information about baptism is found in Paul's personal testimony. In Acts 22:16, Paul recounts that Ananias told him:

> And now why tarriest thou? arise, and be baptized, and wash away thy sins, calling on the name of the Lord.

Notice that Paul was instructed to receive baptism "calling on the name of the Lord." When you were baptized, were you calling in faith on the Lord?

Paul and Peter give us important information about baptism in their epistles. Turning to Romans 6:3-4, we read:

> Know ye not, that so many of us as were baptized
> into Jesus Christ were baptized into his death?
> Therefore we are buried with him by baptism into
> death: that like as Christ was raised up from the
> dead by the glory of the Father, even so we also
> should walk in newness of life.

Similar statements about baptism are found in Colossians 2:12:

> Buried with him [Jesus] in baptism, wherein also ye
> are risen with *him* through the faith of the opera-
> tion of God, who hath raised him from the dead.

Have you died to your old sinful passions? Are you living a new life of Godliness, holiness, and service to others?

Another similar verse is Galatians 3:27:

> For as many of you as have been baptized into
> Christ have put on Christ.

Have you put on the Lord Jesus Christ so that you are like Him? Can you say with Paul "I am crucified with Christ: nevertheless I live; yet not I, but Christ liveth in me" (Galatians 2:20a)?

The last passage we will examine is I Peter 3:21:

> The like figure whereunto *even* baptism doth also
> now save us (not the putting away of the filth of
> the flesh, but the answer of a good conscience to-
> ward God,) by the resurrection of Jesus Christ.

Do you have a clear conscience? Did you at your baptism? Baptism is an answer or witness of a clean conscience. To receive it without a clear conscience can hardly be called anything less than lying.

The Biblical Precedent for Rebaptism

Perhaps after closely examining your heart and the Scriptures, you find that your first baptism was invalid. Some people, when they come to that conclusion, tremble and fear over whether it is right to accept another baptism. "Will I be dishonoring God if I am rebaptized?" they think. Some even wonder whether accepting a second baptism is blasphemy against the Holy Ghost. Please comfort and encourage your heart with the Word of God. Paul once encountered a group of men whose first baptism was insufficient. We read the account of what he did in Acts 19:1-6:

> And it came to pass, that, while Apollos was at Corinth, Paul having passed through the upper coasts came to Ephesus: and finding certain disciples, He said unto them, Have ye received the Holy Ghost since ye believed? And they said unto him, We have not so much as heard whether there be any Holy Ghost. And he said unto them, Unto what then were ye baptized? And they said, Unto John's baptism. Then said Paul, John verily baptized with the baptism of repentance, saying unto the people, that they should believe on him which should come after him, that is, on Christ Jesus. When they heard *this*, they were baptized in the name of the Lord Jesus. And when Paul had laid *his* hands upon them, the Holy Ghost came on them; and they spake with tongues, and prophesied.

Notice that Paul did not hesitate to rebaptize them!

The Anabaptists and Believer's Baptism

The early Anabaptists had much to say about baptism. In a letter to Thomas Müntzer written in 1524, before he himself had received believer's baptism, Conrad Grebel wrote:

> Scripture describes baptism for us as signifying that through faith and the blood of Christ our sins are washed away: to the one baptized that his inner self has been changed, and that he believes, both before and afterward. It signifies that one should be and is dead to sin, and walking in newness of life and spirit; also that he shall certainly be saved by the inward baptism if he lives his faith according to this significance.[11]

Hans Betz, in *Ausbund* hymn #108, wrote:

> From the hearing of Christian teaching, faith does come forth, thereupon baptism is to follow, now that man has received God's Word. The baptism that is in Jesus Christ is a covenant out of a good conscience. Thereafter man is, in this time, to refuse Satan's craftiness. That man henceforth shall live in the will of God, moreover the duty in baptism is, that man shall fulfill His will. Like as a wife is submissive unto her husband here on earth, so one shall be united indeed to Christ the Lord in baptism. Peter says, in the book of Acts: Repent, and be ye baptized on Jesus Christ, it is He, who remits sin, heed this, so receive His promise, the Holy Spirit will be given, whoever believes on Jesus Christ here receives the gift unto life. . . .Listen, child of man, from lust and sin baptism cannot

---

11   Conrad Grebel (Swiss Brethren), "Letter to Thomas Müntzer," 1524; translation from J. C. Wenger, translator, *Conrad Grebel's Programmatic Letters of 1524*, Herald Press, 1970, pp. 29, 31.

wash you, but only gives evidence of purity, this you shall understand in Christ. His righteousness is the garment, which you shall here put on, from all lust, sin, and deception your Adam must be cleansed. . . .Whoever has this baptism is planted into the death of Christ, all his desires thus being crucified, thereby is born anew. This birth has, in Jesus Christ, taken place through water and spirit.[12]

Menno Simons wrote:

This then is the Word and will of the Lord, that all who hear and believe the Word of God shall be baptized as related above. Thereby they profess their faith and declare that they will henceforth live not according to their own will, but according to the will of God. For the testimony of Jesus they are prepared to forsake their homes, possessions, lands, and lives and to suffer hunger, affliction, oppression, persecution, the cross and death for the same; yes, they desire to bury the flesh with its lusts and arise with Christ to newness of life, even as Paul says: Know ye not that so many of us as were baptized into Christ Jesus were baptized into his death? Therefore we are buried with him in baptism into death; that like as Christ was raised up from the dead by the glory of the Father, even so we also should walk in newness of life.

Beloved reader, take heed to the Word of the Lord. Paul who did not receive his Gospel from men, but from the Lord Himself, teaches that even as Christ died and was buried, so also ought we to die unto our sins, and be buried with Christ in baptism. Not

---

12   Hans Betz (Philipite), *Ausbund* #108, c. 1536; translation from *Songs of the Ausbund Vol. 1*, Ohio Amish Library, 1998-2010, pp. 245-246.

that we are to do this for the first time after baptism, but we must have begun all this beforehand, as Paul says: For if we have been planted together in the likeness of his death, we shall also be in the likeness of his resurrection. Knowing this that our old man is crucified with him, that the body of sin might be destroyed, that henceforth we should not serve sin. For he that is dead is freed from sin. For even as Christ has died, has taken away sin, and lives unto God, so true Christians die unto sin and live unto God.[13]

Pilgram Marpeck wrote:

Baptism is an immersion or sprinkling with water desired by the one who is being baptized. Baptism is received and accepted as a sign and co-witness that he has died to his sins and has been buried with Christ; henceforth, he may arise into a new life, to walk, not according to the lusts of the flesh, but obediently, according to the will of God. Those who are thus minded, and confess this intent, should be baptized. When that is done, they are correctly baptized. Then, in their baptism, they will certainly attain forgiveness of sins and thereby, having put on Jesus Christ, they will be accepted into the communion of Christ. The one who is thus baptized experiences this communion, not through the power of baptism, nor through the word that is spoken there, and certainly not through the faith of the godfathers, the sponsors; as his fleshly lusts depart and he puts on Christ, he experiences it through his own knowledge of

---

13   Menno Simons (Dutch Mennonite), *Foundation of Christian Doctrine*, 1539; translation from J. C. Wenger, editor, *The Complete Writings of Menno Simons*, Herald Press, 1984, pp. 121-122.

Christ, through his own faith, through his voluntary choice and good intentions, through the Holy Spirit.[14]

Peter Riedemann wrote:

Therefore we teach that as Abraham was commanded to circumcise in his house, even so was Christ to baptize in his house, as the words that he spoke to John indicate, 'Suffer it to be so, for thus it becometh us to fulfil all God's righteousness.' Now, just as Abraham could not circumcise in his house before the child was born to him, nor all his seed after him, neither can anyone be baptized in the house of Christ unless he be first born of Christ through the word and faith. But he who is born in this manner, is baptized after he hath confessed his faith. History hath proved, likewise, that all the apostles also did this, and we follow them.[15]

Another Hutterite author, Claus Felbinger, wrote:

Baptism makes no one more God-fearing unless he has already a living faith.[16]

Conclusion

The "silent artillery of time" has wrought great damage to the Biblical truth of believer's baptism among some Anabaptist people, and in Christendom as a whole. Believer's baptism is a precious truth which the Apostles handed down and for which our Anabaptist forefathers suffered and died.

---

14   Pilgram Marpeck (Pilgramite), *Judgment and Decision*, c. 1542; William Klassen and Walter Klaassen, editors, *The Writings of Pilgram Marpeck*, Herald Press, 1978, pp. 197-198.

15   Peter Riedemann (Hutterite), *Hutterite Confession of Faith*, 1545; translation from *Confession of Faith*, Plough Publishing, 1970, p. 78.

16   Claus Felbinger (Hutterite); translation from Robert Friedmann, *The Theology of Anabaptism*, Herald Press, 1973, p. 32.

Let us all hold fast to "the faith which was once delivered unto the saints" (Jude 3), including in the area of baptism.

Checklist

Here is a list of the points covered in this chapter for those who desire baptism or are evaluating the validity of their former baptism.

Have you (or did you). . .
- repented?
- confessed your sins?
- received the Word and believed the Gospel?
- called on the Name of the Lord?
- died to your old sinful life?
- risen to a new life of holiness and service to God and others?
- put on Christ?
- If you are considering baptism, is the minister worthy?

Chapter 4

Excommunication

Second. We are agreed as follows on the ban: The ban shall be employed with all those who have given themselves to the Lord, to walk in His commandments, and with all those who are baptized into the one body of Christ and who are called brethren or sisters, and yet who slip sometimes and fall into error and sin, being inadvertently overtaken. The same shall be admonished twice in secret and the third time openly disciplined or banned according to the command of Christ. Mt. 18. But this shall be done according to the regulation of the Spirit (Mt. 5) before the breaking of bread, so that we may break and eat one bread, with one mind and in one love, and may drink of one cup.

—*Schleitheim Confession, Article II*

The early Anabaptists saw clearly that many problems in the churches (Protestant and Catholic) of their day were due to (or at least made worse by) a lack of Scriptural discipline. The Anabaptists used the ban or excommunication (or as Menno Simons sometimes called it, "apostolic exclusion") to keep the church free from false doctrine and sinful lives. Unfortunately, as disputes arose (as they *always* will due to human frailty and the wickedness of our adversary, the Devil), some Anabaptists gave in to the temptation to use the ban as a weapon against each other. It is sad that such actions still continue today among many so-called Anabaptists, while Protestants and Catholics still have (for the most part at least) undisciplined churches. Let us examine the Scriptures to find exactly how the ban is to be used, applied, and what its purpose is.

"He Taketh Away"

Essential to understanding the ban is understanding exactly what is the church? Is it a social club? A place where we go to earn God's favor? A community of close (physical) family who happen to believe the same thing? A place where we learn what to believe? Whenever the New Testament talks about the church, it talks about people—not a building. This is the first important point about the church—Christians do not "go to church." Christians ARE the church. Secondly, a church can lose its status as a church because of sin. If the people are spiritually dead, the church is not a church (see Jesus' words to the Seven Churches in Revelation 2-3). Examining the definition of a Christian gives us the rest of the information we need. Christians are those who have died to their sinful desires and live to God in holiness (Romans 6; I Peter 2:24). Wherever a group of true Christians bond together in brotherly fellowship and continually seek God together, there is a church.

Notice something—the church is a body. This is clearly taught by Paul in I Corinthians 12:12-27:

> For as the body is one, and hath many members, and all the members of that one body, being many, are one body: so also *is* Christ. For by one Spirit are we all baptized into one body, whether *we be* Jews or Gentiles, whether *we be* bond or free; and have been all made to drink into one Spirit. For the body is not one member, but many. If the foot shall say, Because I am not the hand, I am

not of the body; is it therefore not of the body?
And if the ear shall say, Because I am not the eye,
I am not of the body; is it therefore not of the
body? If the whole body *were* an eye, where *were*
the hearing? If the whole *were* hearing, where *were*
the smelling? But now hath God set the members
every one of them in the body, as it hath pleased
him. And if they were all one member, where *were*
the body? But now *are they* many members, yet but
one body. And the eye cannot say unto the hand,
I have no need of thee: nor again the head to the
feet, I have no need of you. Nay, much more those
members of the body, which seem to be more feeble, are necessary: And those *members* of the body,
which we think to be less honourable, upon these
we bestow more abundant honour; and our un-
comely *parts* have more abundant comeliness. For
our comely *parts* have no need: but God hath tempered the body together, having given more abundant honour to that *part* which lacked: That there
should be no schism in the body; but *that* the members should have the same care one for another.
And whether one member suffer, all the members
suffer with it; or one member be honoured, all the
members rejoice with it. Now ye are the body of
Christ, and members in particular.

Notice also Ephesians 4:15-16:

But speaking the truth in love, may grow up into
him in all things, which is the head, *even* Christ:
From whom the whole body fitly joined together
and compacted by that which every joint supplieth,
according to the effectual working in the measure

> of every part, maketh increase of the body unto
> the edifying of itself in love.

However, the universal body of Christ is much larger than any one local body or church. Jesus explained in John 15 how His followers have a relationship to Him analogous to the relationship between a vine and its branches. However, as we know, individual branches of plants can die. Christians can grow weary of the straight and narrow path and give up. Jesus tells us what God the Father, in His infinite wisdom, does in such situations:

> Every branch in me that beareth not fruit he [the
> Father] taketh away. . . .If a man abide not in me,
> he is cast forth as a branch, and is withered; and
> men gather them, and cast *them* into the fire, and
> they are burned (John 15:2a, 6).

God prunes off the vine those who are unfruitful. Just as losing salvation is like being cut off a vine, so being excommunicated by the earthly church can be likened to being amputated from the body (remember, the church is a body). We can conclude that in order for excommunication to work, the church must *be* a body in the first place! This is one of the major shortcomings of many modern American churches—they view church as someplace to go, not as a body of people of which they are a part. If there is a body on an operating table, a skilled doctor can perform an amputation. If there is a scatter of bones on the table, how is he supposed to perform an amputation (excommunication)?

Pilgram Marpeck, writing about how excommunication affects the other members of the body, wrote:

> The other members of the body of Christ experi-
> ence great pain and suffering for at stake is a mem-
> ber of the body of Christ the Lord. They must
> lose a member in order that the other members,

who are well, are not hurt and the whole body destroyed, be it eye, foot, or hand. It should be pulled out or cut off according to the commandment of Christ, our Head: 'If your eye offends you, or your hand, or foot,' etc. The other members of the body of Christ will not be able to do this without great pain and tribulation. If the member is honourable and useful to the body, the tribulation is so much greater. It cannot possibly happen easily or simply. The natural body cannot lose a member without pain. Nor does it immediately cut it off, even if it is failing and weak; rather it uses all kinds of medicines. As long as it is not dead and is only painful, the body bears it with patience and long-suffering, and delays the penalty to allow for improvement. If, however, it allows the body no rest, nor improves by any medicine from the Lord Jesus Christ, through suffering and pain, it must be cut off in order that the other members of the body of Christ remain healthy in the fear and love of God and the neighbor. . .[17]

One reason God gave us excommunication is so that those whom God has separated from the Vine (and those who were mistakenly joined to the local body who were never in the Vine) can be separated from the local body.

Types of Church Discipline

It may come as a surprise to some that there are different forms of excommunication or church discipline for different

---

17   Pilgram Marpeck (Pilgramite), *Judgment and Decision*, c. 1542; translation from William Klassen and Walter Klaassen, editors, *The Writings of Pilgram Marpeck*, Herald Press, 1978, pp. 356-357.

offenses. Let us examine the different forms of excommunication described in Scripture.

Excommunication for Private Offenses

This form of excommunication is discussed by Jesus in Matthew 18:15-18:

> Moreover if thy brother shall trespass against thee,
> go and tell him his fault between thee and him
> alone: if he shall hear thee, thou hast gained thy
> brother. But if he will not hear *thee, then* take with
> thee one or two more, that in the mouth of two
> or three witnesses every word may be established.
> And if he shall neglect to hear them, tell *it* unto
> the church: but if he neglect to hear the church, let
> him be unto thee as an heathen man and a publi-
> can. Verily I say unto you, Whatsoever ye shall bind
> on earth shall be bound in heaven: and whatsoever
> ye shall loose on earth shall be loosed in heaven.

The action which sets off this chain of events is a private, brother-to-brother (or sister) offense—"if thy brother shall trespass against thee." The first step of the procedure is for the wronged brother to go to the offender and let him know "you have trespassed against me." If the offender refuses to repent, the wronged person goes again with one or two others who observe the second meeting. If the offender still refuses to repent, he is given one more opportunity when the issue is brought before the entire local body. If he still refuses to repent, he is excommunicated by the church. He is considered a heathen man in need of having the Gospel preached to him.

Hans Straub, in *Ausbund* #56, wrote:

> If you see him transgress, committing a sin against
> you; kindly you shall beseech him, point out to him

in love between him and you alone. Does he then repent, you shall be satisfied. Will he then not hear you and accept your correction; to another do explain how his affairs took place, and rebuke him again privately. Will he also not hear the two of you, so reveal it to the church. His actions shall indicate if he stands opposed. Will he then submit himself and ask God for grace, so bear Christian patience, do pray to God earnestly for his sin and guilt. Will he not hear the church nor accept her reproof, do explain the evidence, after that let judgment be passed, make known to him God's torment and vengeance if he continues in sin, which will follow after him. From him do separate yourself indeed the very same hour, keep him as a heathen, as Christ has proclaimed. Paul also said without deceit and craftiness, Put him away from among you whoever is disobedient. This love you shall exercise toward your neighbor indeed, neither gossiping nor complaining, if he has done evil, for you have now reproved him, as Christ and Paul teach, otherwise you shall be at fault.[18]

Jakob Ammann wrote:

In regards to brotherly discipline: If a brother sins against another he should be chastised, secretly the first time. If he improves, then he should be forgiven. If he does not improve, then one or two should speak to him and if he then improves, he should be forgiven. If, however, he does not improve, then he should be placed before the congregation. If he then improves, he should also then

---

18   Hans Straub (affiliation unknown), *Ausbund* #56, date unknown; translation from *Songs of the Ausbund Vol. 1*, Ohio Amish Library, 1998-2010, pp. 118-119.

be forgiven. But if he does not want to confess his error and his sins—for indeed all sins, whether small or large, must be confessed—then he should be excommunicated (Matthew 18).[19]

Notice that this procedure is, above all, for *reconciliation*, not for excommunicating or bringing offenders to justice. If at any point in the process the offender repents, the process ends and the repentant man remains in full communion, peace, and harmony with the body. This excommunication process is a method of seeking peace and preserving unity in the church.

Excommunication for Disorderly Life

This form of church discipline is commanded by Paul in II Thessalonians 3:6-15:

> Now we command you, brethren, in the name of our Lord Jesus Christ, that ye withdraw yourselves from every brother that walketh disorderly, and not after the tradition which he received of us. For yourselves know how ye ought to follow us: for we behaved not ourselves disorderly among you; Neither did we eat any man's bread for nought; but wrought [worked] with labour and travail night and day, that we might not be chargeable to any of you: Not because we have not power, but to make ourselves an ensample unto you to follow us. For even when we were with you, this we commanded you, that if any would not work, neither should he eat. For we hear that there are some which walk among you disorderly, working not at all, but are

---

19   Jakob Ammann (Amish), "Long Letter," 1693; translation from John D. Roth, translator, *Letters of the Amish Division: A Sourcebook*, 2nd edition, Mennonite Historical Society, 2002, pp. 32-33.

busybodies. Now them that are such we command and exhort by our Lord Jesus Christ, that with quietness they work, and eat their own bread. But ye, brethren, be not weary in well doing. And if any man obey not our word by this epistle, note that man, and have no company with him, that he may be ashamed. Yet count *him* not as an enemy, but admonish *him* as a brother.

If any man "walketh disorderly," he is to be avoided. What exactly constitutes "walking disorderly"? The context makes it clear: those who are idle busy-bodies who refuse to work, but expect free handouts, are guilty of walking disorderly. We are to withdraw ourselves from such people.

Furthermore, as verses 14-15 show, if anyone refuses to work and/or refuses to observe this excommunication or Paul's other commandments (at least those in II Thessalonians, although it is probably applicable to the other New Testament Scriptures as well), he is to be disciplined with this form of excommunication. We are to have no company with this man, but we are still to admonish him as we would another brother in Christ. We must guard, however, against purely social interaction with him.

The *Hutterite Chronicle* records an occasion where discipline had to be carried out because certain brothers came up with a novel theory related to prayer, and left the rest of the brothers to do more than their share of work.

During the first week of the new year 1629, an unusual matter arose. . .the like of which had never happened before. . .this group separated itself from other brothers and sisters and adopted a peculiar way of praying. They chose unusual times of day to meet for prayer in corners or secretly in the woods, regardless of whether or not their work allowed time for it. They let nothing stop them but insisted that they owed obedience and service to God rather than to men. Three millers. . .held the same opinion and often followed this strange practice instead of running the mill responsibly as they should have done. When they were rebuked, they answered that they had to hold their worship service. They were told that there was a time for prayer and a time for work and running the mill, and besides, it was not necessary for all three to go and pray together. But they were not willing to give up their practice. This going off together and separating themselves from their fellow workers caused division and quarreling. . . .Since their strange practice was hypocrisy and no service to God at all, the whole question was laid before dear brother Valentin Winter, who came immediately with other elders and summoned the three millers and those involved. . . .He appealed to them in different ways and pointed out that while prayer in itself is good and useful, yet everything has its time. . . .If instead of working side by side, someone leaves his brother with all the work and goes off for an hour or two into a corner or into a wood, apparently to pray, and in so doing burdens and annoys his brother, this is no worship of God but a curse.

After all this and more, which cannot all be told, enough had been said to wean these people from their wrong ideas, but not one of them would give in. They all persisted in their opinion and said that God had revealed it to them, that they had had a vision, and that the last day was soon to come. Soon their belief would be proved right. Brother

Valentin and the other servants of the Word and many trusted brothers appealed to them in an earnest and kindly way with words from Scripture and many sound arguments, but to no avail. . .

As they would not accept brotherly correction, the church. . .was called together. When they would not listen to the church either but stubbornly held to their wrong ideas, they were excluded and separated from the church. . . .None of them found repentance but went further astray. Their community soon broke up. . . .And then, as they had to earn their own food and clothing, their hours of prayer soon came to an end.[20]

Excommunication for Heresy

A man may also be disciplined for heresy. Paul told Titus in Titus 3:10-11:

A man that is an heretick after the first and second admonition reject; Knowing that he that is such is subverted, and sinneth, being condemned of himself.

What exactly constitutes heresy, or exactly how the church is to "reject" the unrepentant heretic, I leave to the honest reader to consider. A heretic in the church is to be given two admonitions. If he repents after either one, the procedure ends and he remains in full communion with the congregation. Because Paul directed this command to a minister (Titus), it appears that in most situations, the ministers of the church should lead out in this type of excommunication.

---

20   *The Chronicle of the Hutterian Brethren, Volume 1*, translation published by Plough Publishing House, 1987, pp. 718-720.

Jakob Ammann wrote:

> In regards to heretics: Saint Paul commanded Titus
> in the 3rd chapter to shun an apostate person and
> rabble-rouser if he has been admonished once and
> a second time. Know that such a person is wrong
> and sins as one who has condemned himself. For
> this reason these men were put under the ban so
> that they should be separated and shunned. For
> if someone teaches otherwise and does not sub-
> mit himself to the healing word of our Lord Jesus
> Christ, he is excommunicated and knows nothing.
> Whoever weakens the least of these command-
> ments, and teaches the people so, shall be called
> least [in the Kingdom of Heaven]. All plants that
> were not planted by the heavenly Father through
> His Son will be torn out. Whoever transgresses and
> does not abide in Christ's teaching, that person has
> no God.[21]

Excommunication for Open Carnal Sin

This is perhaps the best known and most debated type of
excommunication. We read in I Corinthians 5:1-5, 9-13:

> It is reported commonly *that there is* fornication
> among you, and such fornication as is not so much
> as named among the Gentiles, that one should
> have his father's wife. And ye are puffed up, and
> have not rather mourned, that he that hath done
> this deed might be taken away from among you.
> For I verily, as absent in body, but present in spirit,
> have judged already, as though I were present, *con-*

---

21   Jakob Ammann (Amish), "Long Letter," 1693; translation from John D.
Roth, translator, *Letters of the Amish Division: A Sourcebook*, 2nd edition, Mennonite Historical Society, 2002, p. 33.

cerning him that hath so done this deed, In the name
of our Lord Jesus Christ, when ye are gathered together, and my spirit, with the power of our Lord
Jesus Christ, To deliver such an one unto Satan for
the destruction of the flesh, that the spirit may
be saved in the day of the Lord Jesus. . . .I wrote
unto you in an epistle not to company with fornicators: Yet not altogether with the fornicators of
this world, or with the covetous, or extortioners, or
with idolaters; for then must ye needs go out of the
world. But now I have written unto you not to keep
company, if any man that is called a brother be a
fornicator, or covetous, or an idolater, or a railer,
or a drunkard, or an extortioner; with such an one
no not to eat. For what have I to do to judge them
also that are without? do not ye judge them that
are within? But them that are without God judgeth.
Therefore put away from among yourselves that
wicked person.

The conditions which begin the procedure of this type of
excommunication are simple. If a person in the church is
openly living in carnal sin, he is to be excommunicated and
shunned. Notice from verses 1-2 that Paul, who was not
present with them, had not simply heard vague rumors about
fornication in the Corinthian congregation. He knew details
about the situation as well as knowing the response of the
other believers. Clearly, this situation had gone on for some
time and was common knowledge in the congregation—
which apathetically tolerated the sinner.

Notice that in the case of such gross and open (known to
the whole or majority of the congregation) sins, no mention
is made of admonishing the sinner and giving him time to
repent. He is simply to be excommunicated. The leaven of

such abominable sin cannot be tolerated in the body for fear of corrupting others by its influence (verses 6-8).

Another point to be noticed is that Paul requires the entire congregation to do the excommunicating. He speaks to the entire congregation as a unit and says that "**ye** are puffed up. . .when **ye** are gathered together. . .To deliver such an one unto Satan." The ministers of the congregation are not kings who decide who is excommunicated and who is readmitted. The entire congregation assents to the judgment of the Word of God concerning the sinner and puts him out. After doing this, each member is then responsible for upholding the shunning of the excommunicated.

Paul spells out the form our separation from the excommunicated must take—refrain from eating with them. Notice that he does not command such avoidance from worldly people involved with the same sins. Therefore, it does not make sense that Paul only means to deny eating Communion to the excommunicated. Are the fornicators and idolaters of the world allowed to partake of our Communion? Of course not. Paul is talking about regular social interaction. The excommunicated should be avoided as much as is practical, with the exception of exhorting them to repentance or caring for them mercifully if they are in dire need. Purely social contact, such as eating a meal together, is not according to Scripture. In the ancient world (and still today), eating a meal with someone is a way of showing peace and harmony. Are we at peace and harmony with those who have apostatized? No! Let us not vainly show peace by eating with them.

Notice, however, that in this most severe and swift form of excommunication, the purpose is still loving: "that the spirit may be saved in the day of the Lord Jesus" (verse 4).

To whom is this form of excommunication applied? Those who are living in the following sins: fornication, covetousness, idolatry, railing on people with abusive language, and extortion. Can others, for instance, those involved in witchcraft or murder, be excommunicated by the church? There is no direct Scriptural word on this. However, we do have another example of Paul applying this type of excommunication.

> Of whom is Hymenaeus and Alexander; whom I have **delivered unto Satan,** that they may learn not to blaspheme (I Timothy 1:20).

Notice that Paul used I Corinthians 5 ("delivered unto Satan") type excommunication against these two. What was their sin? Blasphemy. This sin is not in the list in I Corinthians 5:11. This reference shows that Paul considered this type of excommunication as not limited to just those sins mentioned in verse 11. Another possible reference to this Hymenaeus gives more information about the nature of his blasphemy and the sin for which Paul had excommunicated him.

> And their word will eat as doth a canker: of whom is Hymenaeus and Philetus; Who concerning the truth have erred, saying that the resurrection is past already; and overthrow the faith of some (II Timothy 2:17-18)

Nevertheless, there is never a hint that this type of excommunication can be indiscriminately applied to whatever offense the congregation decides to apply it to. It is excommunication for open, carnal sins of the type listed in verse 11—namely, sins which bar from the kingdom of heaven (see the lists of such sins in Mark 7:21-22, I Corinthians 6:9-10, Galatians 5:19-21, Revelation 21:8, and 22:15). Jakob Ammann wrote:

> All who have love but tell lies, their portion will be in the fiery lake that burns with fire and sul-

phur which is the second death. For the devil is a
liar and a father of lies, and all who knowingly lie
are his servants and ministers. Therefore, without
any prior warning they should be excommunicated
like the others who associate with the works of the
flesh. Saint Paul also says that those who do such
things shall not inherit the Kingdom of God. Such
[people] should also be excommunicated without
any warning, for these are sins unto death and no
one should consider that such people remain in the
congregation and do penance. The ban should ex-
pel from the camp, that is, the church and godly
fellowship, or else the entire congregation would
be worthy of the ban before the Lord.[22]

One question which has puzzled (and unfortunately, divided) Anabaptists over the years is what to do in the case of
a married pair when one of them is excommunicated. Some
have argued that the one member in good standing with the
church should apply shunning to his/her spouse (a practice
called "marital avoidance"), while others have argued that
shunning should not apply in this instance. Unfortunately,
the Bible does not give specific guidance in this circum-
stance. If you find yourself in such a situation, or if you are
advising someone who is, *pray* for heavenly wisdom to do
right. Trust in the Lord to show you what to do.

If the sinner repents after the application of this type of
excommunication and shunning, he is to be accepted back
into full fellowship with the body. Paul instructed the Corinthians, presumably referring to the man who had been excommunicated for fornication, as follows:

---

22   Jakob Ammann (Amish), "Long Letter," 1693; translation from John D.
Roth, translator, *Letters of the Amish Division: A Sourcebook*, 2nd edition, Mennonite Historical Society, 2002, p. 32.

But if any have caused grief, he hath not grieved me, but in part: that I may not overcharge you all. Sufficient to such a man *is* this punishment, which *was inflicted* of many. So that contrariwise ye *ought* rather to forgive *him*, and comfort *him*, lest perhaps such a one should be swallowed up with overmuch sorrow. Wherefore I beseech you that ye would confirm *your* love toward him (II Corinthians 2:5-8).

When the person repents, he is to be readmitted in love. Peter Riedemann wrote:

If, however, one be discovered in the gross and deadly sins of which Paul saith, "If any man that is called a brother be a fornicator, or covetous, or an idolater, or a railer, or a drunkard, or a thief or a robber, with such an one ye must not even eat." Such an one is put out and excluded or separated from the Church without admonition, since the judgment of Paul is already spoken.

And if one is so excluded, we have naught to do with him: have no company with him, that he may be ashamed. Yet is he called to repentance, that perchance he may be moved thereby and return the more quickly to God; and where not, that the Church may remain pure and innocent of his sin, and bear not guilt and rebuke from God on his behalf.[23]

It should be pointed out that with this form of excommunication, as with all others, only individuals are concerned. There is no Biblical command or precedent for the practice of mass excommunication. Excommunication is for the restoration of individuals, not for mass banning of entire groups.

23   Peter Riedemann (Hutterite), *Hutterite Confession of Faith*, 1545; translation from *Confession of Faith*, Plough Publishing, 1970, p. 132.

Why Should We Use the Ban?

What are the reasons we should use the ban? We can see from Scripture two reasons for excommunication.

1. Restoration of the fallen. A man cannot repent until he realizes he has fallen. By excommunicating them, the church helps those who have fallen into continuing sin or heresy to realize their error so they may repent. The church puts them in fact where they are in heart: outside the fellowship and community of the holy saints. This is done, not out of a proud, contentious, arrogant, or holier-than-thou attitude, but out of a spirit of earnest love for a soul gone astray; a spirit seeking the restoration of a wandering sheep. Read the following verses and see the spirit of love and concern for the erring in them:

> that the spirit may be saved in the day of the Lord Jesus (I Corinthians 5:5b)
> Yet count *him* not as an enemy, but admonish *him* as a brother (II Thessalonians 3:15)

Menno Simons wrote:

> If you see your brother sin, then do not pass him by as one that does not value his soul; but if his fall be curable, from that moment endeavor to raise him up by gentle admonition and brotherly instruction, before you eat, drink, sleep, or do anything else, as one who ardently desires his salvation, lest your poor erring brother harden and be ruined in his fall, and perish in his sin. . . .All apostate sisters and brethren. . .[by] their apostasy, rebellious and carnal hatred, they are deprived of grace and the knowledge of God, and become increasingly more wicked, so that they see death in eternal life, and darkness in the heavenly light of divine truth.

Therefore we declare before God and His holy angels that we are clear of their damnable false doctrine, of their sins, obduracy, and eternal death if we have done in vain toward them that which the Lord's Word has commanded us in regard to this matter. We desire not to have communion with them, no lot nor part unto eternity, so long as they do not sincerely renounce their false doctrine and reform their miserable, condemnable, earthly, carnal, and devilish life to the praise of the Lord. But if such things are found in them, in good faith, as before God who sees all things, then we say, Welcome, beloved brethren! Welcome, beloved sisters! And we rejoice beyond measure at the sincere conversion of such brethren and sisters as one rejoices at the restoration of an only son who is healed of a critical and deadly disease, or a lost sheep or penny that is found again, or at the appearance of a son who was given up as lost.[24]

He also wrote:

Observe, brethren, that true evangelical excommunication is an express fruit of unfeigned love, and not a rule of hatred as some altogether erroneously complain and pretend.[25]

2. Church purity. Jesus and the Apostles were concerned about church purity. Sinning members are not to be allowed to remain in the fellowship of the saints. Note the following admonitions:

24   Menno Simons (Dutch Mennonite), *Admonition on Church Discipline*, 1541; translation from J. C. Wenger, editor, *The Complete Writings of Menno Simons*, Herald Press, 1984, pp. 411-414.
25   Menno Simons (Dutch Mennonite), *Account of Excommunication*, 1550; translation from J. C. Wenger, editor, *The Complete Writings of Menno Simons*, Herald Press, 1984, p. 470.

Notwithstanding I have a few things against thee, because thou sufferest that woman Jezebel, which calleth herself a prophetess, to teach and to seduce my servants to commit fornication, and to eat things sacrificed unto idols (Revelation 2:20).

. . .Christ also loved the church, and gave himself for it; That he might sanctify and cleanse it with the washing of water by the word, That he might present it to himself a glorious church, not having spot, or wrinkle, or any such thing; but that it should be holy and without blemish (Ephesians 5:25b-27).

We too should be concerned about church purity.

Your glorying *is* not good. Know ye not that a little leaven leaveneth the whole lump? Purge out therefore the old leaven, that ye may be a new lump, as ye are unleavened. For even Christ our passover is sacrificed for us: Therefore let us keep the feast, not with old leaven, neither with the leaven of malice and wickedness; but with the unleavened *bread* of sincerity and truth (I Corinthians 5:6-8).

If we do not keep leaven out of the church, it will destroy us and the local body. While it is our Heavenly Father's job to keep the Vine pruned, we have been given the responsibility of keeping the congregations pure. Jesus will not do it for us. Read Jesus' admonitions to the churches at Pergamos, Thyatira, Sardis, and Laodicea (Revelation 2:12-29; 3:1-6, 14-22) and notice that Jesus did not take care of their problems for them. He revealed problems to them and told *them* to do something about it.

Pilgram Marpeck wrote:

And again, these same persons [the church] among themselves and before all mankind, shall lead a pure life in united faith and brotherly love to the glory of God, just as Christ asks that His bride (for whom He has given Himself, and whom He has cleansed and betrothed through the baptism of faith and love) be pure and glorious. The Lord's Supper shall also be used to prevent participation of any unbelievers, of unholy false teachers, and of idolatrous or other blasphemous people. Nor will they have any fellowship with Christ's body, regardless of how eloquently and profusely they appeal to Christ's name and consider themselves one with the name of Christ. For what fellowship have the believers (states Paul) with the unbelievers? Or what do light and darkness have in common? (2 Cor. 6:14). . . .Rather, they lead an unclean, disfigured, deceitful life which leads to the shame and chagrin of Christ and His holy church. They move away from the holy, pure, and true faith, and again leave the holy commandments. They shall not have communion with Christ's body nor participate in His supper. They shall be cut off and banned so that the church may remain pure and unblemished so that the entire church not become soiled with the foreign sins of a rascal.[26]

Dirk Philips wrote:

Now this church must be entirely, Eph. 5:27, pure, holy and without blemish, as Paul said. She is the bride, Rev. 19:7, of the Lamb, the Holy City, Rev. 21:2, the New Jerusalem descending from heaven adorned to meet her husband. Such that in her nothing that is unclean can enter, Rev. 21:27, or

---

26 Pilgram Marpeck (Pilgramite), *The Admonition of 1542*, 1542; William Klassen and Walter Klaassen, editors, *The Writings of Pilgram Marpeck*, Herald Press, 1978, p. 296. This book of Marpeck's was actually his adaptation of a work by Bernard Rothmann.

which commits abominations and falsehood, thus only those who truly repent, believe the gospel, hear the living Word of God, receive and keep it, forsaking totally Satan, the anti-christ and the world, renouncing, Matt. 10:39, 16:24, themselves and desiring daily to carry their cross, following Christ in the new birth. . . .But those who on the contrary receive this grace in vain, do not keep it, never produce any fruit by it, walk according to the flesh, cannot enter into the heavenly Jerusalem, but shall have their part outside in the lake of fire. . . .This will happen to all false Christians who have fallen away from the truth (which they have once known and received), Heb. 6:5[f.]; 10:26. In this occasion Jesus Christ has commanded his church and gave to her power to separate from herself all false brothers who break from it by disobedience, to testify that they shall have no part with Christ and all his saints, since they keep persevering in iniquity, Matt. 18:18.[27]

Summary

Misuse of the ban is almost a theme in Anabaptist history. As kingdom Christians, we must leave off this misuse and, in a spirit of love and humility, restore the fallen and keep the church pure in accordance with New Testament commands.

> Brethren, if a man be overtaken in a fault, ye which are spiritual, restore such an one in the spirit of meekness; considering thyself, lest thou also be tempted (Galatians 6:1).

---

27   Dirk Philips (Dutch Mennonite), *Evangelical Excommunication*, c. 1567; translation from Cornelius J. Dyck, William E. Keeney, & Alvin J. Beachy, editors, *The Writings of Dirk Philips*, Herald Press, 1992, pp. 595-596.

Wherefore let him that thinketh he standeth take heed lest he fall (I Corinthians 10:12).

Epilogue—Separation

Several times in the New Testament, we are told to avoid or separate ourselves from certain people. Although these are not excommunication, I have included discussion of two examples below.

Materialistic and Disobedient False Doctrine

We are to separate ourselves from those materialistic persons who hold the false doctrine that the more of this world's goods they have, the more Godly they are. We are also to separate ourselves from those who refuse to accept and consent to the words of the Lord Jesus Christ. Paul told Timothy in I Timothy 6:3-5:

> If any man teach otherwise, and consent not to wholesome words, *even* the words of our Lord Jesus Christ, and to the doctrine which is according to godliness; He is proud, knowing nothing, but doting about questions and strifes of words, whereof cometh envy, strife, railings, evil surmisings, Perverse disputings of men of corrupt minds, and destitute of the truth, supposing that gain is godliness: from such withdraw thyself.

This person is perhaps to be given one admonition (since Paul does say "if any man consent not"), but if he persists in his deceptions, we are to withdraw ourselves from him.

Divisiveness

We must also separate ourselves from those who want to cause divisions contrary to Scripture. Paul tells us in Romans 16:17-18:

> Now I beseech you, brethren, mark them which cause divisions and offences contrary to the doctrine which ye have learned; and avoid them. For they that are such serve not our Lord Jesus Christ, but their own belly; and by good words and fair speeches deceive the hearts of the simple.

We are to "avoid" those who, for other than Scriptural reasons (i.e., separating from a dead, worldly, or sinning church would be Scriptural), want to cause divisions, and those who cause divisions by strange doctrine. These people only serve themselves; the servants of Jesus Christ avoid them.

For as a city without walls and gates, or a field without trenches and fences, and a house without walls and doors, so is also a church which has not the true apostolic exclusion or ban. For it stands wide open to every seductive spirit, to all abominations and for proud despisers, to all idolatrous and willfully wicked sinners, yes, to all lewd, unchaste wretches, sodomites, harlots, and knaves, as may be seen in all the large sects of the world (which however pose improperly as the church of Christ). Why talk at length? According to my opinion, it is the distinguished usage, honor, and prosperity of a sincere church if it with Christian discretion teaches the true apostolic separation, and observes it carefully in solicitous love, according to the ordinance of the holy, sacred Scriptures.[28]

—Menno Simons

---

28   Menno Simons (Dutch Mennonite), *Instruction on Excommunication,* 1558; translation from J. C. Wenger, editor, *The Complete Writings of Menno Simons,* Herald Press, 1984, p. 962.

Chapter 5

Communion

Third. In the breaking of bread we are of one mind and are agreed [as follows]: All those who wish to break one bread in remembrance of the broken body of Christ, and all who wish to drink of one drink as a remembrance of the shed blood of Christ, shall be united beforehand by baptism in one body of Christ which is the church of God and whose Head is Christ. For as Paul points out we cannot at the same time be partakers of the Lord's table and the table of devils; we cannot at the same time drink the cup of the Lord and the cup of the devil. That is, all those who have fellowship with the dead works of darkness have no part in the light. Therefore all who follow the devil and the world have no part with those who are called unto God out of the world. All who lie in evil have no part in the good.

Therefore it is and must be [thus]: Whoever has not been called by one God to one faith, to one baptism, to one Spirit, to one body, with all the children of God's church, cannot be made [into] one bread with them, as indeed must be done if one is truly to break bread according to the command of Christ.

—*Schleitheim Confession, Article III*

The early Anabaptists strenuously rejected the idea of partaking of Communion with Protestants and Catholics. Even when they compromised enough to attend the services of the state churches, they would often leave before Communion was served.[29] Why?

Simply put, being of "one bread" with someone is to acknowledge unity with him. The Anabaptists maintained their separation from church groups which refused to follow Christ in life.

Perhaps this sounds strange and new to you. If so, please read on and earnestly consider the Scriptures given.

One Body, One Bread

This aspect of Communion—that it shows brotherly unity—has been all but forgotten in modern churches. I remember coming across it for the first time in Menno Simons' writings. He wrote:

> Just as natural bread is made of many grains, pul-
> verized by the mill, kneaded with water, and baked
> by the heat of the fire, so is the church of Christ
> made up of true believers, broken in their hearts
> with the mill of the divine Word, baptized with
> the water of the Holy Ghost, and with the fire of
> pure, unfeigned love made into one body. Just as
> there is harmony and peace in the body and all its
> members, and just as each member naturally per-
> forms its function to promote the benefit of the
> whole body, so it also becomes the true and liv-
> ing members of the body of Christ to be one: one
> heart, one mind, and one soul. Not contentious,
> not spiteful and envious, not cruel and hateful, not
> quarrelsome and disputatious one toward anoth-
> er like the ambitious, covetous, and the proud of
> this world. But in all things, one toward another,

29   See John S. Oyer, *"They Harry the Good People Out of the Land,"* Mennonite Historical Society, 2000, pp. 244, 272-273.

long-suffering, friendly, peaceable, ever ready in true Christian love to serve one's neighbor in all things possible: by exhortation, by reproof, by comforting, by assisting, by counseling, with deed and with possessions, yes, with bitter and hard labor, with body and life, ready to forgive one another as Christ forgives and serves us with His Word, life, and death.[30]

When I first read this, I thought it was a strange interpretation, but later found it was firmly rooted in Scripture. Paul explains in I Corinthians 10:14-17:

Wherefore, my dearly beloved, flee from idolatry. I speak as to wise men; judge ye what I say. The cup of blessing which we bless, is it not the communion of the blood of Christ? The bread which we break, is it not the communion of the body of Christ? For we *being* many are one bread, *and* one body: for we are all partakers of that one bread.

Paul explains that just as we partake of one bread in Communion, we as a church are one body. What are some characteristics of a body? As we examine these, ask yourself: does this description fit my church and my relationship to it?

- Each part of a body gives itself for every other part unselfishly, giving its all for the sake of the whole.
- The various parts neither envy nor despise each other, but fulfill their own tasks. "For the body is not one member, but many. If the foot shall say, Because I am not the hand, I am not of the body; is it therefore not of the body? And if the ear shall say, Because I am not the eye, I am not of the body; is it therefore not of the body? If the whole body *were* an

---

30   Menno Simons (Dutch Mennonite), *Foundation of Christian Doctrine*, 1539; translation from J. C. Wenger, editor, *The Complete Writings of Menno Simons*, Herald Press, 1984, pp. 145-146.

eye, where *were* the hearing? If the whole *were* hearing, where *were* the smelling? But now hath God set the members every one of them in the body, as it hath pleased him. And if they were all one member, where *were* the body? But now *are they* many members, yet but one body. And the eye cannot say unto the hand, I have no need of thee: nor again the head to the feet, I have no need of you. Nay, much more those members of the body, which seem to be more feeble, are necessary" (I Corinthians 12:14-22).

• There is no schism, no division, in the body. It is a single, united whole. It moves in the same direction toward the same goal together, and either rejoices or mourns as a single unit. "For our comely *parts* have no need: but God hath tempered the body together, having given more abundant honour to that *part* which lacked: That there should be no schism in the body; but *that* the members should have the same care one for another. And whether one member suffer, all the members suffer with it; or one member be honoured, all the members rejoice with it" (I Corinthians 12:24-26).

This beautiful unity and brotherhood is what we are showing forth when we together partake of one bread and one cup. Hans Schmidt wrote:

With the bread he showed that whoever has his Spirit belongs to him, becomes one flesh with him, a member of his body and of his church community for which he died. Like one bread is made from many grains, and one wine is made from many grapes, all true Christians become one bread and one wine in Christ the Lord. He sustains us and gives us true love in Gemeinschaft [fellowship] with him.[31]

Peter Riedemann wrote:

Christ's love and our love are shown to us in the bread and wine. Just as there are many grains of corn, which are ground by the millstones and become flour, then baked and become bread—and in the bread we no longer distinguish one particle of flour from another—the same thing is true of us human beings, many as we are. When we are ground by the millstone of divine power, believe his word and submit to the cross of Christ, we are brought together, bound with the band of love to one body of which Christ is the head. As Paul puts it, 'We who partake of one bread, though many, are one bread and one body.' Those who truly surrender to the Lord become of one mind, heart, and soul just as the grains of corn unite in the bread; and as Christ, the head, is one with the Father, the members are of one mind with the head as the head also was. As it is written, 'We have the mind of Christ,' but whoever does not have the mind of Christ is not his. And just as each grain of corn gives the others all it has in order that there may be one loaf of bread, Christ our captain has given himself to us as an example that each should love the other as he has loved us, no longer living for himself, but giving his members to live for the whole body and serving the others with the gift he has received so that the body may grow and build itself up. . . .What I have just said about the bread is also true of the wine, for wine is made of many

31   Hans Schmidt (Hutterite), *Ausbund* #55, written before 1537; translation from Peter Hoover, *Secret of the Strength*, Elmendorf Books, 2008, p. 138.

grapes which are crushed in the winepress and then flow together and become wine, and one cannot recognize which grape it comes from. Since Christian unity is likewise proclaimed in the bread and in the whole practice of the Lord's Supper, however, it is not necessary to explain this symbol as well.[32]

Partaking of the Table of the Lord and of Devils?

Someone outside the body of Christ must not be allowed to partake of one bread with the body. Neither should those within the body partake of one bread with those without.

> Ye cannot drink the cup of the Lord, and the cup of devils: ye cannot be partakers of the Lord's table, and of the table of devils. Do we provoke the Lord to jealousy? are we stronger than he? (I Corinthians 10:21-22)

A person clearly giving evidence of an unregenerate life should not be admitted to the Communion table. Let not the unregenerated vainly show unity with the saints. What has Christ to do with Belial? Are the saints one body with the sinner? Is he one body with them? Of course not. Let the sinner not then be of one bread with the saints. Conrad Grebel wrote:

> Although it is simply bread, where faith and brotherly love prevail it shall be partaken of with joy. When observed in that way in the congregation it shall signify to us that we are truly one loaf and one body, and that we are and intend to be true brothers one with another. But if one should be found who is not minded to live the brotherly life, he eats

---

32   Peter Riedemann (Hutterite), *Gmünden Confession*, c. 1530; translation from *Love is Like Fire*, Plough Publishing, 2011, pp. 59-60.

to his condemnation, for he does not discern the difference from another meal. He brings shame on the inward bond, which is love, and on the bread, which is the outward bond. For he fails to be instructed as to the body and blood of Christ and the Testament He made on the cross, that he shall live and suffer for the sake of Christ and the brethren, the Head and the members of Christ. . . .It shall not be observed except in conformity with Christ's rule in Matthew 18, for then it would not be the Lord's Supper, for without Matthew 18 everyone runs after the outward, and that which is inward, namely, love, one lets go; and brethren and false brethren go to the Supper together and eat.[33]

When Jude wrote to the churches, he admonished them about certain carnal sinners in their midst, saying they "defile the flesh, despise dominion, and speak evil of dignities" (Jude 8). He told the churches that "These are spots in your feasts of charity, when they feast with you, feeding themselves without fear" (Jude 12a). Let us keep our communion unspotted from evil persons.

Let a Man Examine Himself

Paul tells us in I Corinthians 11:27-32:

Wherefore whosoever shall eat this bread, and drink *this* cup of the Lord, unworthily, shall be guilty of the body and blood of the Lord. But let a man examine himself, and so let him eat of *that* bread, and drink of *that* cup. For he that eateth and

---

33   Conrad Grebel (Swiss Brethren), "Letter to Thomas Müntzer," 1524; translation from J. C. Wenger, translator, *Conrad Grebel's Programmatic Letters of 1524*, Herald Press, 1970, p. 21, 23 (Grebel numbered each point in this section of his letter; we have omitted the numbers).

drinketh unworthily, eateth and drinketh damnation to himself, not discerning the Lord's body. For this cause many *are* weak and sickly among you, and many sleep. For if we would judge ourselves, we should not be judged. But when we are judged, we are chastened of the Lord, that we should not be condemned with the world.

Before partaking of Communion, we must examine ourselves: "am I right with the body?" Have I envied another member? Have I despised and looked down on another member? Have I given myself unselfishly to helping this body on to God? Have I furthered schism and division in the body? If you find yourself in sin in these areas, make it right before you make yourself of one bread with the body.

Menno Simons wrote:

For all who are earthly and carnally minded, who are not born of God and His Word, who oppose the Lord's Word; love not their neighbor, nor assist him in love: these are not in communion with God, therefore they cannot be kernels of His loaf or guests at His table. For to be carnally minded is death, says Paul. Those who are not born from above, Christ says, cannot see the kingdom of God. Samuel says, Disobedience is as iniquity and idolatry. John says, He that loveth not his neighbor abides in death. Again, he that loveth not knows not God, for God is love. In brief, without love it is all in vain that we believe, baptize, celebrate the Lord's Supper, prophesy, and suffer.

Therefore we admonish all those who desire to celebrate this Supper that they learn rightly to know what the true Supper is, what it signifies, how and whereunto it is to be used, and who are to be partakers of it. And then also to examine themselves well, as Paul teaches, before they eat of this bread and drink of this cup lest they comfort themselves with the visible sign and come short of the reality represented by the sign. For they who know not Christ and His righteousness, do not believe Him and His Word, nor walk therein, but walk according to the superstitious doctrine and commands of men: when they nevertheless partake of the Lord's table, they eat and drink damnation to themselves.[34]

Taking Communion with Other Congregations

After examining this Biblical truth, it should be clear that it would be wrong to partake of Communion in a church composed largely (if not entirely) of unregenerated people. If the people are not regenerated, do not make yourself of one bread with them!

Menno Simons wrote:

Christ left with His church the Holy Supper, in bread and wine, as a remembrance of His death. . . .Is a Christian now permitted to observe the deviating, errant, papal, daytime meal, and neglect the Lord's nighttime meal?[35] Judge for yourselves since Paul says ye cannot be partakers of the Lord's table and partakers of the table of Antichrist and the devil. I Cor. 10:21. If we cannot partake of both, then

---

34   Menno Simons (Dutch Mennonite), *Foundation of Christian Doctrine*, 1539; translation from J. C. Wenger, editor, *The Complete Writings of Menno Simons*, Herald Press, 1984, p. 149.
35   Dutch *Nachtmaal* – the early Anabaptists observed the Lord's Supper at night.

we must neglect one or the other. Well, then, keep
your distance![36]

Dirk Philips wrote:

> . . .we maintain that this Supper shall not be held
> except only with the friends of God, the true
> Christians, who have accepted the gospel and
> through it have improved themselves, and upon
> the confession of their faith are correctly baptized
> in the name of the Father, the Son, and the Holy
> Spirit, Matt. 28:19, [those who] are truly concerned
> in their faith to walk as Christians, and earnestly
> reflect upon conformity to Christ, his suffering
> and death, his burial and resurrection. In summa-
> ry, [those] who are one body with Christ and all
> the saints—these and no others are according to
> the evidence of the gospel to be renewed, admon-
> ished, and established with this Supper in the fel-
> lowship of Christ and all the saints.[37]

Conclusion

Examine yourself and your church body and ask yourself if
you experience the reality of one body which partaking of
one bread witnesses. If not, there is a problem!

---

36   Menno Simons (Dutch Mennonite), *Admonition to the Amsterdam
Melchiorites*, 1539; translation from J. C. Wenger, editor, *The Complete Writings of Menno Simons*, Herald Press, 1984, p. 1025.
37   Dirk Philips (Dutch Mennonite), *Enchiridion*, c. 1564; translation from
Cornelius J. Dyck, William E. Keeney, & Alvin J. Beachy, editors, *The Writings
of Dirk Philips*, Herald Press, 1992, p. 128.

Oh, delightful assembly and Christian marriage feast, commanded and ordained by the Lord Himself! Here no carnal pleasures, the flesh, and appetites, but the glorious and holy mysteries, by means of the visible signs of bread and wine, are represented to and sought by true believers.

Oh, delightful assembly and Christian marriage feast, where take place no improper and shameful mockery, and no senseless songs; but the pious Christian life, peace, and unity among all the brethren. The joyous word of divine grace moreover, His glorious benefits, favor, love, service, tears, prayers, His cross and death, are set forth, and urged with delightful thanksgiving and devout joy.

Oh, delightful assembly and Christian marriage feast to which the impenitent and proud despisers are, according to Scripture, not invited: the harlots, rogues, adulterers, seducers, robbers, liars, defrauders, tyrants, shedders of blood, idolaters, slanderers, etc., for such are not the people of the Lord. But they are invited who are born of God, true Christians who have buried their sins, and who walk with Christ in a new and godly life. They are invited who crucify the flesh and are driven by the Holy Spirit; who sincerely believe in God, seek, fear, and love Him, and in their weakness willingly serve and obey Him, for they are members of His body, flesh of His flesh, bone of His bone.

Oh, delightful assembly and Christian marriage feast, where no gluttonous eating and drinking are practiced, nor the wicked vanity of pipes and drums is heard; but where the hungry consciences are fed with the heavenly bread of the divine Word, with the wine of the Holy Ghost, and where the peaceful, joyous souls sing and play before the Lord.[38]

—Menno Simons

---

38   Menno Simons (Dutch Mennonite), *Foundation of Christian Doctrine*, 1539; translation from J. C. Wenger, editor, *The Complete Writings of Menno Simons*, Herald Press, 1984, p. 148.

Chapter 6

Separation from the World

Fourth. We are agreed [as follows] on separation: A separation shall be made from the evil and from the wickedness which the devil planted in the world; in this manner, simply that we shall not have fellowship with them [the wicked] and not run with them in the multitude of their abominations. This is the way it is: Since all who do not walk in the obedience of faith, and have not united themselves with God so that they wish to do His will, are a great abomination before God, it is not possible for anything to grow or issue from them except abominable things. For truly all creatures are in but two classes, good and bad, believing and unbelieving, darkness and light, the world and those who [have come] out of the world, God's temple and idols, Christ and Belial; and none can have part with the other.

To us then the command of the Lord is clear when He calls upon us to be separate from the evil and thus He will be our God and we shall be His sons and daughters.

He further admonishes us to withdraw from Babylon and the earthly Egypt that we may not be partakers of the pain and suffering which the Lord will bring upon them.

From all this we should learn that everything which is not united with our God and Christ cannot be other than an abomination which we should shun and flee from. By this is meant all popish and antipopish works and church services, meetings and church attendance, drinking houses, civic affairs, the commitments [made in] unbelief and other things of that kind, which are highly regarded by the world and yet are carried on in flat contradiction to the command of God, in accordance with all the unrighteousness which is in the world. From all these things we shall be separated and have no part with them for they are nothing but an abomination, and they are the cause of our being hated before our Christ Jesus, Who has set us free from the slavery of the flesh and fitted us for the service of God through the Spirit Whom He has given us.

Therefore there will also unquestionably fall from us the unchristian, devilish weapons of force—such as sword, armor and the like, and all their use [either] for friends or against one's enemies—by virtue of the word of Christ, Resist not [him that is] evil.

—*Schleitheim Confession, Article IV*

Some modern Anabaptists have the idea that separation from and nonconformity to the world can be reduced to an equation, such as:

black felt hat + cape dress + horse & buggy = separate from the world

long sleeves + no television + no smoking = separate from the world

The Bible does teach the practicing of distinctives, such as modest dress (I Timothy 2:9-10; I Peter 3:3-5; Jude 1:23), which clearly and visibly separate the saint from the world. However, separation from the world is *much more* than this. As the early Anabaptists rightly saw, separation is largely the product of a redeemed life. Holy living will separate the saint from the whole evil world. If we do not realize this, what (precious little) is left of our "separation" and "noncon-formity" will be lost.

We must not make the error of putting the cart before the horse, and we must also avoid presenting a beautifully writ-ten envelope which has no contents. If our separation and nonconformity does not begin right, not only will it not end right, but it must also be a stench and abomination before God.

> The sacrifice of the wicked *is* an abomination to the LORD: but the prayer of the upright *is* his de-light (Proverbs 15:8).

A Peculiar People

There are only two kinds of people in all the earth: those fol-lowing Satan and those following Jesus; those of the world and those of the kingdom of God. Peter tells us in I Peter 2:9-10:

> But ye *are* a chosen generation, a royal priesthood, an holy nation, a peculiar people; that ye should shew forth the praises of him who hath called you out of darkness into his marvelous light: Which in time past *were* not a people, but *are* now the people of God: which had not obtained mercy, but now have obtained mercy.

We as Christians have *by nature* a certain separation from the world. Just as sheep are by nature separate from goats, Christians are separate from the world. Christians have ex-perienced the new birth (a radical transformation of heart and life, given by God Himself); the world at large has not. It is that simple. Without this separation from the world, all other separation is meaningless because, if there is no new birth, then the person—no matter how "plain"—is still a part of the world because he has not been regenerated.

We must begin separation from the world here. Until by the new birth we have joined the peculiar people, the holy nation, other separation is make-believe, a false assurance, and a lie to the watching world.

Peter Riedemann wrote:

> Here it is evident that God at the beginning separated and sundered the devout from the godless. Of these he saith that the Holy Spirit will not dwell in them who are subject to sin; with the others, however, he promiseth to be at all times and to be their God if they zealously keep his commandments, teaching and ways, as we see especially in the case of Abraham, who was called the father of all believers. . . .For even as God the Lord, who is God over all gods, is separate from all idols, as he himself saith, "To whom then will ye liken me or what likeness will ye compare unto me, for I declare beforehand things that have not yet come to pass." And of Christ, Paul saith, "What concord hath Christ with Belial?" In the same way will he have his people separate, because the believer hath no part with the unbeliever. . . .And further, he saith, "Depart ye, depart ye, go ye out from thence, touch no unclean thing; go ye out of the midst of her; purify yourselves, ye that bear the vessels of the Lord." And further, "Come out from among them, my people, and be ye separate," saith the Lord, "and touch no unclean thing; and I will receive you and will be a Father unto you and ye shall be my children." And again, "Come out of her, my people, that ye be not partakers of her sins, and that ye receive not of her plagues."

For as he is holy and, as is said above, apart from all abomination, even so will he have his people sundered from the assembly of godless men, that they may be to him an holy people, as it is written, "Ye shall be holy; for I the Lord your God am holy."[39]

Peter Walpot wrote:

We do not condemn anyone (would much rather save one if possible), since no human being can do this, but the evil works of each one condemn him. But likewise as the Apostle Paul says, when Noah prepared the ark to the saving of his household and through the ark condemned the world, so still today all those who follow Christ and the Church of believers (which bears the likeness of the ark), condemn this world by going out from and separating from it with the testimony that its works are evil and that if they do not repent they will not become heirs of salvation.[40]

Love Not the World

After possessing separation in *kind*, we can move on to separation in *heart*, *thought*, and *attitude*.

John tells us:

Love not the world, neither the things *that are* in the world. If any man love the world, the love of the Father is not in him. For all that *is* in the world, the lust of the flesh, and the lust of the eyes, and the pride of life, is not of the Father, but is of the world. And the world passeth away, and the lust

39   Peter Riedemann (Hutterite), *Hutterite Confession of Faith*, 1545; translation from *Confession of Faith*, Plough Publishing, 1970, pp. 139-140, 144.
40   Peter Walpot (Hutterite), "Letter to Simon the Apothecary," 1571; translation from Robert Friedmann, "Reason and Obedience," *Mennonite Quarterly Review* (January 1945), p. 32.

thereof: but he that doeth the will of God abideth
for ever (I John 2:15-17).

We must *love not* the world. No matter how "plain" a man
is, it is all to no avail if he is chafing at separation and longing and lusting after the world. Do you love the world? A
person cannot love the world and love God. Pray to God
as the hymn writer did—"Take my love, my Lord I pour/at
Thy feet its treasure-store." Pour your love at God's feet and
leave none for the world. Such a heart position is essential to
being correctly separated from the world.

An *Ausbund* hymnwriter wrote from prison:

> Therefore love not the world, nor that which is
> in the world, gold, silver, possessions, and money,
> thereto the lust of the flesh. For all this will pass
> away, but the Word of the Lord shall endure for-
> ever.[41]

Peter Walpot wrote:

> Between the Christian and the world there exists a
> vast difference like that between heaven and earth.
> The world is the world, always remains the world,
> behaves like the world and all the world is noth-
> ing but world. The Christian, on the other hand,
> has been called away from the world. He has been
> called never to conform to the world, never to be a
> consort, never to run along with the crowd of the
> world and never to pull its yoke. The world lives ac-
> cording to the flesh and is dominated by the flesh.
> Those in the world think that no one sees what
> they are doing; hence the world needs the sword.
> The Christians live according to the Spirit and are
> governed by the Spirit. They think that the Spirit

---

41   Unknown Philipite, *Ausbund* #120, c. 1536; translation from *Songs of the Ausbund Vol. 1*, Ohio Amish Library, 1998-2010, p. 296.

sees what they are doing and that the Lord watches them. Hence they do not need and do not use the sword among themselves. . . .To sum up: friendship with the world is enmity with God. Whosoever, therefore, wishes to be a friend of the world makes himself an enemy of God (James 4:4). If to be a Christian would reside alone in words and an empty name, and if Christianity could be arranged as it pleases the world; if, furthermore, Christ would permit what is agreeable to the world, and the cross would have to be carried by a sword only. . . .then both authorities and subjects—in fact, all the world—would be Christians. Inasmuch, however, as a man must be born anew (John 3:7), must die in baptism to his old life, and must rise again with Christ unto a new life and Christian conduct, such a thing cannot and shall not be: "It is easier," says Christ, "for a camel to go through the eye of a needle than for a rich man (by whom is meant here the authorities in particular) to enter the kingdom of God or true Christianity" (Matthew 19:24).[42]

All That is In the World

The next step in nonconformity is recognizing what is worldly. The Apostle John gives us a definition of "the world":

For all that *is* in the world, the lust of the flesh, and the lust of the eyes, and the pride of life, is not of the Father, but is of the world (I John 2:16).

Anything which caters to the lust of the flesh, feeding man's desire for a pleasurable bodily feeling or sensation; the lust of the eyes, feeding his desire for visual stimulation; or the

---

42   Peter Walpot (Hutterite), *Great Article Book*, 1577; translation from Robert Friedmann, *The Theology of Anabaptism*, Herald Press, 1973, p. 39.

pride of life, feeding his desire for applause or recognition, is of the world and its god, Satan.

After crucifying these lusts in his own heart, the man can now move on to visible, recognizable separation and non-conformity.

> I beseech you therefore, brethren, by the mercies of God, that ye present your bodies a living sacrifice, holy, acceptable unto God, *which is* your reasonable service. And be not conformed to this world: but be ye transformed by the renewing of your mind, that ye may prove what *is* that good, and acceptable, and perfect, will of God (Romans 12:1-2).

What are some ways a man can be separated from the world in practice, after being separated from it in kind and in heart? The separate man refuses to conform to the world in many areas.

- *Dress.* He wears humble, unostentatious clothing which neither attracts attention to himself (feeding his pride of life) nor exposes his body to the view of others (feeding their lust of the eyes). This applies to both men and women. Brethren, let us not allow people to know our loyalties only by the way our sisters are dressed. Let us dress separate as well. Being separate in dress also means refusing to follow fashion. It seems that even in "plain" churches, there are definite fashions which begin, spread, end, and are replaced. The things such fashions consist of are not always wrong in and of themselves, but must we spend valuable time and energy following fashion (imitating the world, by the way) when there is so much work to be done in the kingdom of God? Let us leave fashion behind forever!

- *Home life.* While others let their children do as they please, he brings his children up in the fear of the Lord (Ephesians 6:4). He works to provide for his family while his wife is his helpmeet and a keeper at home (Titus 2:5). He welcomes into his home all the children who the Lord blesses him with (Psalm 127:3-5).

- *Morality.* While those of the world feed the lust of the flesh and eyes on each other incessantly, he keeps his mind, body, and heart pure, feeding on the Word of God (Philippians 4:8).

- *Transportation.* While the world chases after bigger, flashier, louder, and more powerful vehicles, he buys what is within his means and will serve his purposes without show.

- *Thinking.* While the world teaches evolution, he believes what the Bible says about creation. While the world ridicules the Bible, he still believes and trusts God's Word. While the world is obsessed with saving whales and great apes, he is obsessed with the salvation of souls.

- *Speech.* While the world cusses, swears, takes God's Name in vain, and tells dirty jokes and stories nonstop, he keeps his speech clean as Jesus did. "And all bare [Jesus] witness, and wondered at the gracious words which proceeded out of his mouth" (Luke 4:22a). "Let your speech *be* alway with grace, seasoned with salt, that ye may know how ye ought to answer every man" (Colossians 4:6).

- *Music.* He avoids and despises the heathenish country, rock, pop, rap, etc. music of the world and the "Christian" music tainted by these styles. He listens to and sings music which glorifies God. "Speaking to

yourselves in psalms and hymns and spiritual songs,
singing and making melody in your heart to the Lord;
Giving thanks always for all things unto God and the
Father in the name of our Lord Jesus Christ" (Ephesians 5:19-20).

- *Eating.* While the world stuffs itself and makes itself
  fat as others starve (feeding the lust of the flesh), he
  eats what he needs to live and shares with others.

- *Money.* While the world chases after uncertain rich-
  es and seeks security in retirement accounts and the
  stock market, he gives to others in need and stores
  up treasure in heaven rather than on earth (Matthew
  6:19-21).

- *Rulership.* While "The kings of the Gentiles exercise
  lordship over them" (Luke 22:25a), among the kingdom of God there is neither carnal lordship in the
  church nor political entanglement with the kingdoms
  of this world (II Timothy 2:4).

- *Self-defense.* He allows the Lord to protect him rather
  than taking up the sword to defend himself (Matthew 5:38-48; 10:16; 26:52).

- *Divorce.* While the world sees marriage as temporary
  and expendable, he is faithful to his marriage vows
  until death (his or his spouse's).

- *Attitude.* While the world does everything with a "me
  first" attitude, he has a gracious attitude of serving
  others. "Jesus Christ. . .gave himself for us, that he
  might redeem us from all iniquity, and purify unto
  himself a peculiar people, zealous of good works"
  (Titus 2:13b-14).

Behold, this is a picture of a man truly separate from the
world!

No Alliance

Christians must go yet further in separation from the world:
We must have no alliance with the world. The Apostle Paul
wrote:

> Be ye not unequally yoked together with unbeliev-
> ers: for what fellowship hath righteousness with
> unrighteousness? and what communion hath light
> with darkness? And what concord hath Christ with
> Belial? or what part hath he that believeth with an
> infidel? And what agreement hath the temple of
> God with idols? for ye are the temple of the living
> God; as God hath said, I will dwell in them, and
> walk in *them*; and I will be their God, and they shall
> be my people. Wherefore come out from among
> them, and be ye separate, saith the Lord, and touch
> not the unclean *thing*; and I will receive you, And
> will be a Father unto you, and ye shall be my sons
> and daughters, saith the Lord Almighty (II Corin-
> thians 6:14-18).

We must have no alliance (unequal yoke) with those who
use worldly methods, have worldly goals, or worldly intents.
Righteousness and unrighteousness have no fellowship or
communion with each other. Light and darkness cannot be
mixed. God and Satan do not cooperate. The temple of God
has no part with idols. Our bodies, being the temple of God
Himself, must be kept pure from idols. God has issued this
call to separation, giving a promise with it: "I will receive
you, And will be a Father unto you, and ye shall be my sons
and daughters." This promise is for those who obey the call:
"Wherefore come out from among them, and be ye separate. . .and touch not the unclean *thing*."

A Swiss Brethren Anabaptist wrote:

> Thus we see that Christ has really placed the sheep-fold (i.e., his holy church) into the violent realm of wolves. Therefore, his flock will never have peace with the world—unless they are robbed of their right eye by the Ammonite King Nahash. Sela (Jn. 10; Gal. 4; Mt. 10, 23; Lk. 12, 21; 1 Sam. 11).
>
> For Christ's church is spiritual, whereas the world is carnal; the church can therefore not live in peace with the world. As soon as peace with the world begins, for Christians, the peace of Christ comes to an end (Rom. 8; Jn. 15, 16; Gal. 1; Jas. 4).[43]

The Hutterite chronicler wrote:

> The world hated and persecuted us solely for the sake of Christ's name and his truth, because we followed him, and for no other reason. And this was a sure sign: If someone traveled with only a staff in his hand to show that he did not mean to harm anyone, or if he prayed before eating, he was called an Anabaptist,[44] a heretic. Such is the stupidity of the devil. But if someone became unfaithful and walked according to the ways of the heathen, a sword at his side and a musket at his shoulder, from that moment on he was welcome to the world and "a good Christian" in their eyes.
>
> A man who wore no ruff round his neck or other signs of vanity in his attire, who declared that gambling, haughtiness, gluttony, drunkenness, and

---

43   Unknown Swiss Brethren, Preface to *Golden Apples in Silver Bowls*, c. 1630. Quoted from *Golden Apples in Silver Bowls: The Rediscovery of Redeeming Love (1999)*, p. 63, courtesy of Lancaster Mennonite Historical Society, 2215 Millstream Road, Lancaster, Pa.

44   The early Anabaptists despised being called "Anabaptists" – rebaptizers. They pointed out that if infant baptism was not true baptism and they baptized upon confession of faith, then they were not *re*-baptizing.

carousing are evil and against God, and conducted himself in a quiet way with patience and other qualities befitting a disciple of Christ—such a person was reckoned by the world to be a heretic, a sectarian, a deceiver, or a fool. He was hated and despised by people who had never seen him before and could accuse him of no wrongdoing, since he had harmed no one and had no wish to do so. This just shows what the world has come to.

But as soon as someone was unfaithful, returned to the world, and stepped into the inn saying, "Boys, let me treat you to a drink," singing immoral songs, drinking wildly with others, and sticking a plume in his hat like a fool; as soon as he indulged in gambling and dancing, wearing a huge ruff round his neck, baggy breeches, and clothes with ornamental slits, making a show of their thousand and one much-honored sacraments, spreading syphilis and other dreadful diseases, and swearing and blaspheming God—from that moment on such a person was befriended by the world and acknowledged again as one of them. They approved of him and said, "Well done! You were right to leave the brothers and be converted and become a good Christian. Now that you have the true faith never let yourself be led astray from our church again. You did well to leave the brothers and separate yourself from their sect"—as they call us. Wherever he went, he found good friends. People liked him and accepted him, even if they had never seen him before. They could see all his wicked deeds and vices, and still he was liked by the world because he had forsaken the truth of God. From all this it is clear that they hate

and persecute us simply because we are zealous for
God. Envy, stemming from the old serpent, is behind their hatred of God's truth. No one wants to
admit it, but there is no denying it.[45]

Worldly Churches

Most churches today have opened their doors to the world.
In great honor and esteem, the world is given a comfortable
place in the church. Mr. Worldly-Wiseman, Mr. Leave-
Nothing-Behind, Mr. Please-the-Flesh, Mr. Explain-it-Away,
and Mr. Embrace-Sin present soft messages pleasing to the
seared consciences of the members of the worldly church.
Despite their claim to be Christians, if there is no fruit
showing their claim to be true, we must separate ourselves
from them as from the rest of the world.

> If any man teach otherwise, and consent not to
> wholesome words, *even* the words of our Lord Je-
> sus Christ, and to the doctrine which is according
> to godliness. . .from such withdraw thyself (I Tim-
> othy 6:3, 5b).

Pilgram Marpeck wrote:

> We are to avoid and separate ourselves from those
> who do not believe the Word, until they repent.
> Then we are to receive them in love and patience.[46]

Hans Landis, the last of the Swiss Brethren to be executed in
Switzerland (he was killed in 1614), told some state church
ministers on the day of his death:

> since you do not live and walk according to the
> teachings of Christ and His Apostles, I do not

45   *The Chronicle of the Hutterian Brethren, Volume 1,* translation published
by Plough Publishing House, 1987, pp. 408-409.
46   Pilgram Marpeck (Pilgramite), *Aufdekung der Babylonischen Hürn,* 1544;
translation from Peter Hoover, translator, *The Triumph, Peace, and Power of
True Christianity,* Benchmark Press, 2001, p. 18.

want you, nor do I need you: I do not desire you.
In all of thirty years I have never wanted to attend
your services because you do not lead a better life
and walk.[47]

Jakob Ammann wrote that he had warned against attending
the services of the state churches,

> Just as the Lord Jesus also warned his disciples
> to guard themselves against the teachings of the
> Pharisees. Christ also spoke through Saint John:
> My sheep hear my voice. They do not follow
> a strange voice, rather they flee from it for they
> do not know the voice of the stranger. For when
> someone among the people of Israel went to a for-
> eign prophet, he was supposed to die. Therefore,
> it is not fitting for us to run away from the church
> of God to a foreign teacher as if one could find
> light in darkness or the truth among lies. If one
> wants to hear liars talk, then one can go to the state
> church.[48]

Isolationism?

Separation from the world is not isolationism. It is comfortable to bask in the fellowship of holy brethren and let the
world sin outside, but this is not what Jesus has called us to
do all of the time. We are not simply supposed to enjoy the
kingdom of God, we are supposed to expand it! We do not do
this by political action and trying to force the world to obey
the laws of God's kingdom, but by recruiting individuals.
Those individuals who are willing to surrender to God, expe-

---

47   Hans Landis (Swiss Brethren), 1614; translation from James Lowry,
translator and editor, *Hans Landis*, 2003, Ohio Amish Library, p. 143.
48   Jakob Ammann (Amish), "Long Letter," 1693; translation from John D.
Roth, translator, *Letters of the Amish Division: A Sourcebook*, 2nd edition, Mennonite Historical Society, 2002, p. 40.

rience the new birth, forsake their sin, and live the kingdom
life with their brethren, should be brought in.

Menno Simons wrote:

> . . .the whole world with its spirit, doctrine, sac-
> rament, worship, and conduct are quite diverse
> from Christ's Spirit, Word, sacrament, worship, and
> example, and are alas nothing but a new Sodom,
> Egypt, and Babylon. Rev. 11:8. . .all who confess
> God's Word and partake of His Spirit are called
> to let their light shine, to give light to the world, to
> reprove all wickedness with word, deed, life, and
> death, and to confess the Lord's holy name, Word,
> and will and to confirm it with a pious and unblam-
> able life according to the Scriptures.[49]

Separation from Amusements and Entertainment

It has been said that worldly amusements are as natural to
worldlings as the joy of the Lord is to Christians.[50] It could
be added that the opposite is also true—the joy of the Lord
is just as foreign to worldlings as worldly amusements are to
Christians. What has the Christian in common with the spirit
of the theater, the television, the plays, and amusements of
this world? The near-nudity of the beaches and fairs? The
carnal pleasures? Nothing! Stand aloof, my brethren and sisters! There is nothing there for us.

Nevertheless, the question "then what does the church
have to offer for us?" is a fair question. In my study of the
Bible, I have never noticed a place where God commands

---

49   Menno Simons (Dutch Mennonite), *Foundation of Christian Doctrine*,
1539; translation from J. C. Wenger, editor, *The Complete Writings of Menno
Simons*, Herald Press, 1984, p. 181.

50   See *The Historical Journal*, Vol. X, No. 1.

us to give something up without giving us something better. Here are some things God has given us in place of worldly entertainments.

1. God gave us good ways to accomplish recreation without worldly amusements. One is enjoying the beautiful world of nature which He created. Another is enjoying family members.

2. God has also created the church for us. The church is so much better than the fairs, clubs, and amusements of the world! My brethren, it is wonderful to be in the fellowship of saints! What can compare with the joy of seeking God's face together? Nevertheless, church is not all about having a good time together. Some have fallen for that error and instead of separating themselves from the amusements of the world, they have simply reproduced them in the context of the church. This is not separation! The church is about seeking God and His kingdom while pressing Heavenward together. It is not about amusing ourselves. There is nothing wrong with enjoying each other's company, but when Christianity becomes a social event, there is not much Christianity left.

3. Another thing God has given us in place of worldly amusements is service. Why should we fill our time with the empty, vain, useless, soul-parching evil of the worldly fairs, theaters, movies, TV, etc. when God's kingdom is chronically short of enthusiastic workers? Is there anything more fulfilling than serving others? All born again Christians have spiritual gifts which God wants us to use to build His kingdom! Let us not bury our

gifts in the earth while "enjoying" the unfulfilling nonsense of the world.

Holier Than Thou?

Some people object to being visibly nonconformed (especially in dress) by saying that dressing differently will give people the impression that we are unapproachable, proud, or arrogant, and they will stay away. In my experience, the opposite is true. I cannot count how many times people have asked some member of my family "Are you Amish or Mennonite?" What an opportunity to witness is provided!

However, it is possible to have a proud, arrogant attitude which *does* repel people. It is also abhorrent to God.

> I have spread out my hands all the day unto a rebellious people, which walketh in a way *that was* not good, after their own thoughts. . .Which say, Stand by thyself, come not near to me; for I am holier than thou. These *are* a smoke in my nose, a fire that burneth all the day (Isaiah 65:2, 5).

Brethren and sisters, let us not have a holier than thou attitude. Such an attitude repels seekers, is abhorrent to God, and is itself worldly (pride of life). Let us forsake it.

Separated Unto!

Many groups have been—or at least, thought they were— separated from the world, but that is not enough. We cannot simply be separated *from* the world; we must be separated *to* God. Separation from the world is not separation simply for separation's sake. We must be separated from the world because the spirit of the world and its fruits are opposed to the Spirit of God and His fruits. Thus, if the Holy Spirit inhabits us and we are submitted to God's will, we are GOING to be different from the world—without question. The world will bring forth its evil fruit in its children and God will bring forth His holy fruit in His children—and the two will be strikingly different!

> For all that *is* in the world, the lust of the flesh, and
> the lust of the eyes, and the pride of life, is not of
> the Father, but is of the world (I John 2:16).

Conclusion

Holy brethren, let us embrace and propagate the *entire* doctrine of nonconformity and separation. If we do not keep the whole, what is left will soon be lost.

> No man that warreth entangleth himself with the
> affairs of *this* life; that he may please him who hath
> chosen him to be a soldier (II Timothy 2:4).

God's kingdom is waiting to be built. Let us lay aside all worldly attitudes and actions forever and please Him who has called us to be soldiers for His kingdom.

"For whatsoever is born of God overcometh the world: and this is the victory that overcometh the world, *even* our faith."

(I John 5:4)

Chapter 7

Shepherds in the Church

Fifth. We are agreed as follows on pastors in the church of God: The pastor in the church of God shall, as Paul has prescribed, be one who out-and-out has a good report of those who are outside the faith. This office shall be to read, to admonish and teach, to warn, to discipline, to ban in the church, to lead out in prayer for the advancement of all the brethren and sisters, to lift up the bread when it is to be broken, and in all things to see to the care of the body of Christ, in order that it may be built up and developed, and the mouth of the slanderer be stopped.

This one moreover shall be supported of the church which has chosen him, wherein he may be in need, so that he who serves the Gospel may live of the Gospel as the Lord has ordained. But if a pastor should do something requiring discipline, he shall not be dealt with except [on the testimony of] two or three witnesses. And when they sin they shall be disciplined before all in order that the others may fear.

But should it happen that through the cross this pastor should be banished or led to the Lord [through martyrdom] another shall be ordained in his place in the same hour so that God's little flock and people may not be destroyed.

—*Schleitheim Confession, Article V*

ne of the main grievances the early Anabaptists had with the state churches was the poor selection of leaders. Qualified, holy men should be the only ones put in the office of "shepherd" (elder or bishop). That office, although it has a cross associated with it, is a very blessed office and one of the highest positions of servanthood possible. Let us preserve a right view of shepherds in the church.

It is probably not a universal, hard-and-fast rule, but there is a common thought that a church—particularly small churches—can rise no higher than its leaders. In large measure, what the leaders are, the church will be. This emphasizes the urgent need to choose Godly leaders absolutely committed to Jesus Christ who are determined to serve Him.

Ministers Must Be Qualified

It may sound so simple as to hardly need mentioning, but before a man is ordained to be a minister, he must be Biblically qualified for the office. A good place to start is to keep certain people out of the church in the first place. Numerous times the Scriptures contain lists of people who will not enter heaven. If any such person wants to be admitted to the body, he must have demonstrated his repentance from such evil works. The following is a list of such sins, compiled from Mark 7:21-22, I Corinthians 6:9-10, Galatians 5:19-21, Revelation 21:8, and 22:15.

- Evil thoughts
- Adultery
- Fornication
- Murder
- Foolishness
- Covetousness
- Extortion
- Contention
- Strife
- Envy
- Unbelief
- Theft
- Covetousness
- Wickedness
- Deceit
- Idolatry

- Drunkenness
- Witchcraft
- Jealousy
- Sedition
- Reveling
- Lasciviousness
- Evil eye
- Blasphemy
- Pride
- Homosexuality
- Reviling
- Hatred
- Wrath
- Heresy
- Fearfulness

No one who is guilty of these sins and refuses to repent and forsake them should be admitted into the fellowship of God's holy children. Is this raising the standard too high? Is it too radical? I believe not, for this is what the Word of God teaches. This is not sinless perfection nor is it never falling into the sins mentioned, but is a life of victory over sin (I John 1:8-2:1)!

Keeping these people from our membership by never admitting them will go a *long* way toward having Godly leaders. Thankfully, however, God has not left us in the dark about what qualifies a man for leadership in the church. This list is compiled from I Timothy 3:1-7 and Titus 1:5-9. I encourage my readers to read both of these passages in their entirety. Notice that an elder/bishop *must* have **all** of these qualifications—none are optional.

- Blameless
- Vigilant
- Given to hospitality
- Not given to wine
- Not greedy after money
- Not a brawler
- Rules well his own house
- Having faithful children
- Not soon angry
- Lover of good men
- Just
- Holy
- Self-controlled
- Holding fast the faithful word
- Able to convince gainsayers
- Sober
- Good conduct
- Apt to teach
- Not a striker
- Patient
- Not covetous
- Not a novice
- Not self-willed
- Husband of one wife (women and unmarried men are not qualified)

We should carefully scrutinize every candidate for eldership to ensure that he meets the qualifications given in Scripture.

A Swiss Brethren Anabaptist – possibly Hans Hotz – said:

> A Christian community must be pure and holy. If she detects gifts and virtues in a member as Paul speaks about it, then she has the authority to send them to preach the gospel. . . .Before there can be Christian preaching there must first be a change of life, improvement, and the new birth. Then, if the virtues are detected in such a person, the commissioning follows as Christ called the apostles to follow him. They had to become subject to his righteousness and abstain from sin. Only then he sent them and commanded them to preach the good news.[51]

51   ?Hans Hotz (Swiss Brethren), 1538; translation from Walter Klaassen, editor, *Anabaptism in Outline*, Herald Press, 1981, p. 125.

Menno Simons wrote:

> Behold, dearest friends, thus the ministers should be minded who serve the Lord's church, that they may not hear from the obstinate and obdurate, Why do you teach others and not yourselves? Nor can they teach otherwise to the glory of God, for the service of the New Testament is a service of the Spirit and not of the letter. II Cor. 3:6. Therefore Christ never chooses as laborers in His vineyard, as servants and builders, such as are avaricious and drunkards; in order that His servants might teach the kingdom of God, which is spiritual, in purity of heart, shepherding the sheep of Christ, not by force, but gently, not seeking filthy lucre, but with a kindly disposition, not as those who seek dominion of others, but as examples to the flock of Christ, not serving for a certain benefice, pension, or salary as do your teachers, but solely for the gain of the souls which Christ Jesus has so dearly bought with His precious blood.
>
> They look wholly to God (who by His grace, created, delivered, regenerated, and sent them to His service) for their daily needs, diligently supporting themselves as much as is possible by the grace of the Lord, from their own or their rented farm, or from working at their trade; lest they be found selling the free Word of God which was given them without price, and living on shameful gain, robbery, and theft. Let all sincere and pious servants of Christ beware of this, and whatever they cannot earn by due labor and diligence will doubtlessly be provided for them as needed, not by the impenitent heathen, the drunkards, the usurers, the forni-

cators, but by the converted brethren who fear the Lord, for whom they sow spiritual things. For such teachers are the oxen which tread out the corn and are not to be muzzled (I Cor. 9:9; I Tim. 5:18; Deut. 25:4); men who are worthy of double honor, with whom all things should be shared, and who shall live by the Gospel according to the Lord's own ordinance, as the priests under the law lived by the altar. These are the true laborers who are worthy of their hire, as Christ says. Such teachers we shall acknowledge, honor, and maintain in love. And for their labors' sake we keep peace with them, as Paul says, For they watch for your souls as they that must give account. Heb. 13:17.[52]

Peter Riedemann wrote:

If the Church needeth one or, indeed, more ministers, she must not elect them as pleaseth herself, but wait upon the Lord to see whom he chooseth and showeth them. Therefore they should continue in earnest prayer and petition to God that he might care for them, answer their need and show them whom he hath chosen for his ministry. After continuing thus earnestly in prayer, those who have been recognized through God's counsel to be suitable are presented to all. . . .None, however, is confirmed in his office except he be first proved and revealed to the Church, and have the testimony of a good life and walk, lest he fall into the snare of the wicked.[53]

---

52   Menno Simons (Dutch Mennonite), *Brief Confession on the Incarnation*, 1544; translation from J. C. Wenger, editor, *The Complete Writings of Menno Simons*, Herald Press, 1984, p. 442.

53   Peter Riedemann (Hutterite), *Hutterite Confession of Faith*, 1545; translation from *Confession of Faith*, Plough Publishing, 1970, pp. 80-81.

The Responsibilities of an Elder

What responsibilities does an elder carry? Here are a few roles elders play in a Scriptural church:

Teaching. The qualifications of an elder state that he must be "apt to teach."

Rebuking. Elders have the responsibility to rebuke if necessary (II Timothy 4:2).

Watch the flock. They are to guard their congregations like a shepherd guards his sheep (Hebrews 13:17; I Peter 5:1-3). They should vigilantly watch for and faithfully warn against deception, sin, and Satan's tactics.

He does not lord over his flock. Although he is in authority, he is not to press his point and use psychological coercion (I Peter 5:3). He leads by example and should be able, by Biblical reasoning, to persuade his flock to go this way or that. However, he should not be lax when it comes time to practice discipline.

Menno Simons wrote:

> Where the Spirit of God constrains to preach, there the Word will be taught unsullied in the power of the Spirit, and genuine children of the Spirit will be begotten thereby. But where flesh and blood constrains, there a carnal doctrine is taught, and carnal disciples are begotten. For that like produces like is incontrovertible. . . .The Scriptures teach plainly that a preacher rightly called must teach the Word of God without perverting glosses, without the admixture of leaven, as Peter says: If any man speak, let him speak as the oracles of God. I Pet. 4:11. They who are the children of the Holy Ghost speak the word of the Spirit, as Christ said, It is not ye that speak, but the Spirit of your Father which

speaketh in you. Matt. 10:20. For he whom God
hath sent speaketh the word of God. John 3:34.[54]

The Elder and His Congregation

It is the responsibility of the congregation to take the elders
seriously. In order for the elders to be able to fulfill their responsibilities, the congregation must be willing to be taught,
entreated, rebuked, and watched over. They must be willing
to submit themselves to the elders—not unconditionally, of
course, but in light of the Word of the Lord and knowing
that often the elders know much more than most members
do about many situations. Most elders would also greatly
appreciate words of encouragement from their congregation.
They want to know that they are appreciated.

> And we beseech you, brethren, to know them
> which labour among you, and are over you in the
> Lord, and admonish you; And to esteem them very
> highly in love for their work's sake. *And* be at peace
> among yourselves (I Thessalonians 5:12-13).
>
> Obey them that have the rule over you, and submit
> yourselves: for they watch for your souls, as they
> that must give account, that they may do it with joy,
> and not with grief: for that *is* unprofitable for you
> (Hebrews 13:17).

Peter Riedemann wrote:

> The voice of those whom God draws, teaches, and
> sends is heard by the hearts of believing people.
> They do not speak their own words but God's,
> so men gladly listen to them and follow his word
> not only with their ears, but with their hearts. Je-

---

54   Menno Simons (Dutch Mennonite), *Foundation of Christian Doctrine*,
1539; translation from J. C. Wenger, editor, *The Complete Writings of Menno
Simons*, Herald Press, 1984, p. 164.

sus says, 'My sheep hear my voice; they do not listen to the voice of a stranger. I go before them, and they follow me, for I know who are mine, and they know me.' From this we can recognize that up till now many—indeed all—have run without being sent by God, and have not been shepherds of the sheep, but hirelings who sought their own gain more than that of the sheep. As no betterment results from their preaching, they have not proclaimed God's word but their own fabrication (even though their deceit was covered up with godly words). That is why the sheep did not hear them. For when God's word is proclaimed in its purity, it will not return empty but will accomplish all that is commanded it, says the Lord. As Christ wanted to send to his sheep shepherds who would faithfully pasture them, he said to them, 'Go out into all the world, preach and proclaim the Gospel'—that is, the good news about him and what good things he has done for us.[55]

Money

There are great dangers with a salaried ministry. First, there is no New Testament precedent for such a practice. Second, there is a danger of the hireling not caring for his congregation the way an unpaid minister, working purely out of love, would. Thirdly, there is a danger of the hireling looking at the ministry as a job or business ("Perhaps I will be a doctor, or maybe a lawyer, or perhaps a minister?"). Fourthly, the hireling will be tempted to refrain from preaching the whole counsel of God for fear of being turned out of his pulpit or

---

55   Peter Riedemann (Hutterite), *Gmünden Confession*, c. 1530; translation from *Love is Like Fire*, Plough Publishing, 2011, p. 31.

having his wages reduced. Fifthly, there will be a temptation to only be a minister for the sake of the money, in which case the hireling is not even qualified for the ministry, since he would love filthy lucre. Let us not put hirelings in our pulpits. Menno Simons wrote:

> O my faithful reader, ponder this. As long as the world distributes splendid houses and such large incomes to their preachers, the false prophets and deceivers will be there be by droves.
>
> All heresy, seduction, idolatry, tyranny, drunkenness, pomp, pride, and hypocrisy can by their methods be defended with Scripture; as also their improper and scandalous belly-serving and care-free life, which the ignorant and blind world believes to be right.[56]

Nevertheless, even though a salaried ministry is not wise, it *is* the congregation's responsibility to provide for the financial welfare of its ministers.

> Let the elders that rule well be counted worthy of double honour, especially they who labour in the word and doctrine. For the scripture saith, Thou shalt not muzzle the ox that treadeth out the corn. And, The labourer *is* worthy of his reward (I Timothy 5:17-18).
>
> Do ye not know that they which minister about holy things live *of the things* of the temple? and they which wait at the altar are partakers with the altar? Even so hath the Lord ordained that they which preach the gospel should live of the gospel (I Corinthians 9:13-14).

---

56   Menno Simons (Dutch Mennonite), *Reply to Gellius Faber*, 1554; translation from J. C. Wenger, editor, *The Complete Writings of Menno Simons*, Herald Press, 1984, p. 663.

A Word of Encouragement

In conclusion, I want to pass on to all dedicated, holy ministers a word of encouragement from our beloved brethren, Peter and Paul.

> Having then gifts differing according to the grace that is given to us, whether prophecy, *let us prophesy* according to the proportion of faith; Or ministry, *let us wait* on *our* ministering: or he that teacheth, on teaching; Or he that exhorteth, on exhortation: he that giveth, *let him do it* with simplicity; he that ruleth, with diligence; he that sheweth mercy, with cheerfulness (Romans 12:6-8).

> And when the chief Shepherd shall appear, ye shall receive a crown of glory that fadeth not away (I Peter 5:4).

Chapter 8

The Sword

Sixth. We are agreed as follows concerning the sword: The sword is ordained of God outside the perfection [completeness, fullness] of Christ. It punishes and puts to death the wicked, and guards and protects the good. In the Law the sword was ordained for the punishment of the wicked and for their death, and the same [sword] is [now] ordained to be used by the worldly magistrates.

In the perfection of Christ, however, only the ban is used for a warning and for the excommunication of the one who has sinned, without putting the flesh to death,— simply the warning and the command to sin no more.

Now it will be asked by many who do not recognize [this as] the will of Christ for us, whether a Christian may or should employ the sword against the wicked for the defense and protection of the good, or for the sake of love.

Our reply is unanimously as follows: Christ teaches and commands us to learn of Him, for He is meek and lowly in heart and so shall we find rest to our souls. Also Christ says to the heathenish woman who was taken in adultery, not that one should stone her according to the law of His Father (and yet He says, As the Father has commanded me, thus I do), but in mercy and forgiveness and warning, to sin no more. Such [an attitude] we also ought to take completely according to the rule of the ban.

Secondly, it will be asked concerning the sword, whether a Christian shall pass sentence in worldly dispute and strife such as unbelievers have with one another. This is our united answer: Christ did not wish to decide or pass judgment between brother and brother in the case of the inheritance, but refused to do so. Therefore we should do likewise.

Thirdly, it will be asked concerning the sword, Shall one be a magistrate if one should be chosen as such? The answer is as follows: They wished to make Christ king, but He fled and did not view it as the arrangement of His Father. Thus shall we do as He did, and follow Him, and so shall we not walk in darkness. For He Himself says, He who wishes to come after me, let him deny himself and take up his cross and follow me. Also, He Himself forbids the [employment of] the force of the sword saying, The worldly princes lord it over them, etc., but not so shall it be with you. Further, Paul says, Whom God did foreknow He also did predestinate to be conformed to the image of His Son, etc. Also Peter says, Christ has suffered (not ruled) and left us an example, that ye should follow His steps.

Finally it will be observed that it is not appropriate for a Christian to serve as a magistrate because of these points: The government magistracy is according to the flesh, but the Christians' is according to the Spirit; their houses and dwelling remain in this world, but the Christians' are in heaven; their citizenship is in this world, but the Christians' citizenship is in heaven; the weapons of their conflict and war are carnal and against the flesh only, but the Christians' weapons are spiritual, against the fortification of the devil. The worldlings are armed with steel and iron, but the Christians are armed with the armor of God, with truth, righteousness, peace, faith, salvation and the Word of God. In brief, as is the mind of Christ toward us, so shall the mind of the members of the body of Christ be through Him in all things, that there may be no schism in the body through which it would be destroyed. For every kingdom divided against itself will be destroyed. Now since Christ is as it is written of Him, His members must also be the same, that His body may remain complete and united to its own advancement and upbuilding.

—*Schleitheim Confession, Article VI*

𝔄nabaptists are well-known for nonresistance. Unfortunately, some modern Anabaptists are falling for a perverted doctrine of "peace" or "pacifism" while others have lost nonresistance altogether. In the meantime, I wonder whether other churches—which have neither compromised nor abandoned the doctrine—really grasp its fullness and splendor.

Definition of Nonresistance

We will begin by asking "what exactly is nonresistance?" Nonresistance is defined by the teachings of Jesus and the Apostles. Ponder the following verses.

> Ye have heard that it hath been said, An eye for an eye, and a tooth for a tooth: But I say unto you, That ye resist not evil: but whosoever shall smite thee on thy right cheek, turn to him the other also. And if any man will sue thee at the law, and take away thy coat, let him have *thy* cloke also. And whosoever shall compel thee to go a mile, go with him twain. Give to him that asketh thee, and from him that would borrow of thee turn not thou away. Ye have heard that it hath been said, Thou shalt love thy neighbour, and hate thine enemy. But I say unto you, Love your enemies, bless them that curse you, do good to them that hate you, and pray

for them which despitefully use you, and persecute you; That ye may be the children of your Father which is in heaven: for he maketh his sun to rise on the evil and on the good, and sendeth rain on the just and on the unjust. For if ye love them which love you, what reward have ye? do not even the publicans the same? And if ye salute your brethren only, what do ye more *than others?* do not even the publicans so? Be ye therefore perfect, even as your Father which is in heaven is perfect (Matthew 5:38-48).

For we wrestle not against flesh and blood, but against principalities, against powers, against the rulers of the darkness of this world, against spiritual wickedness in high *places.* Wherefore take unto you the whole armour of God, that ye may be able to withstand in the evil day, and having done all, to stand (Ephesians 6:12-13).

Then said Jesus unto him, Put up again thy sword into his place: for all they that take the sword shall perish with the sword (Matthew 26:52).

He that leadeth into captivity shall go into captivity: he that killeth with the sword must be killed with the sword. Here is the patience and the faith of the saints (Revelation 13:10).

(See also Luke 6:27-36; II Corinthians 10:3-5; II Timothy 2:24-26). From these verses we clearly see two sides of the doctrine of nonresistance. First, the nonresistant person will not harm his enemy. He will not take a gun and fight for his country; he will not fight to protect his property, life, or family. He does not harm his enemy.

Secondly, he loves his enemy. He actively shows and demonstrates care and concern for his enemy. If his enemy is hungry, the nonresistant man feeds him. If he is thirsty, the nonresistant man offers him a drink. By so doing, he brings conviction on his enemy and may be the human means of bringing him to repentance and salvation. In this, he has more than conquered his enemy. If he had killed his enemy, he would not have changed his foe at all—he would simply have removed him from the world. Such a victory, if victory it is, would be a hollow one indeed. However, if by my kindness and love he is brought to repentance, then indeed I have conquered him through love.

Consider Peter Riedemann's definition of love:

> Love cannot hide itself because its nature is light. It must shine and show itself in active work, serving all men and doing good. For love does everyone good. It is ready to serve; it is kind, gentle, mild, patient, humble, pure, temperate, modest, sympathetic, brotherly, warm-hearted, good, compassionate, gracious, lowly, forbearing, loyal, and peaceable. Love is not repulsive; it is not proud, puffed up, boastful, envious, or drunken; it is not self-willed, disobedient, deceitful, quarrelsome, or thieving. Love does not gossip; it is not jealous, irate, or spiteful, it despises no one, but bears all things and suffers all things; it is not revengeful; it does not repay evil with evil; it does not rejoice in what is wrong, but rejoices in truth. Only love does God's work.[57]

In brief, "love worketh no ill to his neighbour" (Romans 13:10) but rather does him good.

---

57   Peter Riedemann (Hutterite), *Gmünden Confession*, c. 1530; translation from *Love is Like Fire*, Plough Publishing, 2011, p. 25.

Conrad Grebel wrote:

> One should also not protect the gospel and its adherents with the sword, nor themselves. . . .True believing Christians are sheep among wolves, sheep for the slaughter. They must be baptized in anxiety, distress, affliction, persecution, suffering, and death. They must pass through the probation of fire, and reach the Fatherland of eternal rest, not by slaying their bodily [enemies] but by mortifying their spiritual enemies. They employ neither worldly sword nor war, since with them killing is absolutely renounced.[58]

Peter Riedemann wrote:

> Now since Christ, the Prince of Peace, hath prepared and won for himself a kingdom, that is a Church, through his own blood; in this same kingdom all worldly warfare hath an end, as was promised aforetime, "Out of Zion shall go forth the law, and the word of the Lord from Jerusalem, and shall judge among the heathen and shall draw many peoples, so that they shall beat their swords into ploughshares and their lances or spears into pruning hooks, sickles and scythes, for from thenceforth nation shall not lift up sword against nation, nor shall they learn war any more."
>
> Therefore a Christian neither wages war nor wields the worldly sword to practice vengeance, as Paul also exhorteth us saying, "Dear brothers, avenge not yourselves, but rather give place unto the wrath of God, for the Lord saith, Vengeance is mine; I will repay it." Now if vengeance is God's and not

---

58 Conrad Grebel (Swiss Brethren), "Letter to Thomas Müntzer," 1524; translation from J. C. Wenger, translator, *Conrad Grebel's Programmatic Letters of 1524,* Herald Press, 1970, p. 29.

ours, it ought to be left to him and not practiced or exercised by ourselves. For, since we are Christ's disciples, we must show forth the nature of him who, though he could, indeed, have done so, repaid not evil with evil. For he could, indeed, have protected himself against his enemies, the Jews, by striking down with a single word all who wanted to take him captive. . .

Since, as it is said above, all temporal things are foreign to us and naught is our own, a Christian can neither strive, quarrel nor go to law on their account; on the contrary, as one whose heart is turned from the world and set upon what is divine, he should suffer wrong; as Paul saith, "Now therefore there is utterly a fault among you because ye go to law one with another. Why do ye not rather take wrong? Why do ye not rather suffer yourselves to be defrauded?" Thus, since Christians must not sue one another at law, going to law and sitting in judgment are completely done away with among Christians.[59]

Why Must We Be Nonresistant?

There are four reasons why we must practice nonresistance.

The example of Christ. It is undeniable that Jesus lived a nonresistant life. We are to be like Him, including in this area. The Apostle Peter instructs us to follow in Jesus' steps and applies this principle specifically to nonresistance: "For even hereunto were ye called: because Christ also suffered for us, leaving us an example, that ye should follow his steps: Who did no sin, neither was guile found in his mouth:

---

59   Peter Riedemann (Hutterite), *Hutterite Confession of Faith*, 1545; translation from *Confession of Faith*, Plough Publishing, 1970, p. 108, 112-113.

Who, when he was reviled, reviled not again; when he suffered, he threatened not; but committed *himself* to him that judgeth righteously: Who his own self bare our sins in his own body on the tree, that we, being dead to sins, should live unto righteousness: by whose stripes ye were healed" (I Peter 2:21-24).

Jakob Hutter wrote:

> Rather than knowingly wrong a man to the value of a penny, we would let ourselves be robbed of a hundred florins; rather than strike our worst enemy with the hand—to say nothing of spears, swords, and halberds as the world does—we would let our own lives be taken.
>
> As anyone can see, we have no physical weapons, neither spears nor muskets. No, we want to show by our word and deed that men should live as true followers of Christ, in peace and unity and in God's truth and justice.[60]

The commands of Christ and the Apostles. The commands quoted previously show conclusively that we are instructed to live nonresistantly.

The Spirit of Christ. "Now if any man have not the Spirit of Christ, he is none of his" (Romans 8:9b). If my heart is not conformed to Christ's so that I have a Christ-like spirit, then I am not a true Christian. Part of Jesus' spirit is nonresistance; we are to follow Him in it. Part of Jesus' spirit is meekness and lowliness (Matthew 11:29); we are to follow Him in it. Many things can be tested by that "meek and lowly" criterion. Does a meek and lowly spirit send a person running like a madman across a war-torn battlefield, shooting every "enemy" human being in sight? Does it send him

---

60   Jakob Hutter (Hutterite), "Letter to Ferdinand I," 1535; translation from *Brotherly Faithfulness: Epistles from a Time of Persecution*, Plough Publishing, 1979, pp. 69-70.

to the back yard to tear around on an ATV for nothing but the amusement and thrill of the flesh? Does it send him to the grandstands of some sporting event to scream and yell because some man has successfully taken a pigskin across a field, or raced a car madly around a circle track faster than the rest?

An example of nonresistant love may draw the offender to repentance. The Apostle Paul wrote, "Therefore if thine enemy hunger, feed him; if he thirst, give him drink: for in so doing thou shalt heap coals of fire on his head. Be not overcome of evil, but overcome evil with good" (Romans 12:20-21). Proverbs 16:7 says, "When a man's ways please the LORD, he maketh even his enemies to be at peace with him."

Peter Riedemann wrote:

> But whoever wants to strive for perfection is obliged, in order to reach this goal, to love all who hate and despise him as well. For Christ taught, "to the men of old it was said, 'You shall love your friend and hate your enemies,' but I say to you love your enemies. . .that you may be children of your Father in heaven, who makes his sun rise over the evil and the good and sends rain on the just and the unjust." For that is God's way: through patience he calls sinners to repentance. So the children who have received his Spirit should walk in its footprints and be disciples of God. Paul teaches, "Be followers of God as beloved children." Through patience and through returning good for evil, they should point their enemy to uprightness, for it is written, "If your enemy is hungry, feed him; if he is thirsty, give him drink, for in so doing you will heap fiery coals on his head." Perhaps this kindness may af-

fect him so that he considers deeply and turns over a new leaf. He will think, "I treat this man badly, and he repays me with kindness and does all he can to serve me and is my friend. Oh, what am I doing? I want to change and do as he does—leave the evil and pursue the good, for what does it help me to live in wickedness and oppose the will of God?" When this takes place—when you move a human being to have a good conscience—you have helped a soul from death to life, which is sure to be rewarded by God. Where this does not take place—where God sees you repay evil with good—he will say in his heart (even though he does not let it be seen), "This man accepts everything patiently that I maliciously do to him, and is so ready to do good to me—he is truly better than I am." In this way your well-doing becomes a witness to him. Such love is a band of perfection. But if he does not better himself and repent after such a witness, he increases God's wrath upon him in the day of judgment. When love takes hold of a man, he is pleasing to God and approved by man.[61]

"Peace"?

Some today have fallen for a perverted doctrine of "peace", searching for world peace *through political action.*

Such people fail to realize what nonresistance truly is. Jesus gave His teachings to individuals to implement in their own lives, not to regulate the actions of the kingdoms of this world. The kingdoms of this world are provided with the sword to keep order (Romans 13:4). Jesus' kingdom is

---

61   Peter Riedemann (Hutterite), *Gmünden Confession*, c. 1530; translation from *Love is Like Fire*, Plough Publishing, 2011, pp. 21-24.

not of this world—governments can neither participate in nor legislate in the kingdom. In addition, Jesus clearly told us that war will continue until He returns (Matthew 24:6; Mark 13:7; Revelation 17:14). Furthermore, the kingdoms of this world are under the dominion of Satan (Matthew 4:8, 9; Luke 4:5-7; John 12:31; 14:30; II Corinthians 4:4). Let us not vainly try to make Satan's dominion less hellish; let us strive to bring individuals out of his kingdom and into the kingdom of God!

Pilgram Marpeck, in discussing the irreconcilable differences between true Christians and political power and the sword, wrote:

> God has appointed no power or rulers on the earth except Caesar. Caesar and his worldly government will rule on the earth until their time is up, as predicted by Daniel (Dan. 11), when the wrath of God will come upon all men (Isa. 24). Until then all flesh needs the power and control of Caesar.
>
> Jesus Christ, on the other hand, does not rule or judge in earthly inheritances or in earthly kingdoms. No matter whether his followers receive good or evil, they pay back nothing but patience and love. They are willing to submit everything they have, even their bodies and their lives, to earthly powers. That is everything, except their true faith in Christ. . .
>
> To know Christ and his teaching is to live not after the flesh. It is not to hang onto our possessions, but to be born again, through which we die to all earthly things. He who hangs onto his old life and possessions will lose them. But he who gives them up comes to possess eternal life (Matt. 16, 19). He puts (Luke 9) every thought of self-defense behind

his back, offers to carry the cross for his master
and Lord, Christ, and does this faithfully with all
meekness, love, and patience (Matt. 11) as a lamb
of God.

We protect ourselves against the enemies of Christ
by becoming more than conquerors through him.
Our triumph, not limited by time, is eternal (Rom.
8; 1 John 5). Christ says, 'Rejoice! I have overcome
the world' (John 16). Overcoming power never
comes from winning in an earthly conflict. Whoever wins a conflict is overcome sooner or later by
a stronger opponent who dominates him. That is
because earthly conflicts are not won with Christ.
It is the flesh that wins them, and the flesh with its
triumphs passes away. . .

The selfish also try to justify themselves with love
for their neighbors. They ask: 'Shouldn't we defend
our neighbors when they are in danger, if we can
do so? Hasn't God made us responsible to do this?
God told us not to ignore our neighbors when they
are in need, and to treat others like we want them
to treat us' (Matt. 7).

Using such human logic, Simon Peter took it upon
himself to defend Christ. But listen to what Christ
did: He reached out and healed the man whom
Peter, using worldly force, had struck (Luke 22).
Christ does not want the kind of love that causes
others to get hurt or despised. Rather, he wants
to see us loving and not hating our worst enemies
(Luke 6), no matter what they do to us. . .

True Christians help those whom they can, whether friend or foe, as long as no one gets hurt by their
help. The spirit of brotherly assistance will never

be wanting among them. In fact, Christ's followers are so dedicated to helping others that they would be ready to die for them. Complete love in Christ reaches out to friends and enemies. It is the result of freedom in Christ and spiritual union with him. . .

In Christ, the only sword we know is the sword of the Word. It is the sword through which we judge and are judged, and it is the only sword we are commanded by Christ to use. We are to avoid and separate ourselves from those who do not believe the Word, until they repent. Then we are to receive them in love and patience. This is the true Christian's judgment in this time. They are not asked by Christ to judge in any other way.[62]

Practical Applications

We often think of conscientious objection to war and not shooting attackers as applications of nonresistant principles. These are excellent applications; however, there are many others. We will here discuss two which were mentioned in the Schleitheim Confession.

Jury Duty

Can a Christian sit on a jury? The purpose of jury duty is to sit in judgment over the temporal affairs of this life. Is this part of the business of a Christian?

No. The civil government has been placed over such matters. By participating in their affairs by performing jury duty, I would be showing affinity with them. Such affinity will

---

62   Pilgram Marpeck (Pilgramite), *Aufdekung der Babylonischen Hürn*, 1544; translation from Peter Hoover, translator, *The Triumph, Peace, and Power of True Christianity*, Benchmark Press, 2001, pp. 3-4, 6-7, 11, 18.

never exist between the kingdom of God and the kingdoms of this world. Let the world judge its own matters.

Second, if it is not lawful for a Christian to sue at the law, but rather take wrong (I Corinthians 6:1-8), and if when someone else tries to sue him he is to do his utmost to keep the matter out of court (Matthew 5:40), then is it consistent for him to sit in judgment in a court of law?

Thirdly, if it is wrong for a Christian to kill, is it lawful for him to participate in sentencing a man to death?

Fourthly and finally, Jesus has left us an example.

> And one of the company said unto him, Master, speak to my brother, that he divide the inheritance with me. And he said unto him, Man, who made me a judge or a divider over you? And he said unto them, Take heed, and beware of covetousness: for a man's life consisteth not in the abundance of the things which he possesseth (Luke 12:13-15).

Can a Christian Be a Government Official?

For a Christian to be a government official would be mixing the kingdoms—which does not work. Either he will cling to the methods of the kingdom of God or he will cling to the methods of the kingdoms of this world. He cannot do both. Being a government official will almost certainly require him to use the sword, and at the very least will require him to be part of an organization (the government) which has been entrusted with the sword (Romans 13:4)—all while professing to be a Christian, a member of a group of peaceful people who have been disarmed with Peter, hearing the words "Put up again thy sword into his place: for all they that take the sword shall perish with the sword" (Matthew 26:52).

Again, Jesus has left us an example:

> When Jesus therefore perceived that they would
> come and take him by force, to make him a king,
> he departed again into a mountain himself alone
> (John 6:15).

Jesus would not be made an earthly king. Let us follow Him.

Conclusion

We have mentioned two sides of nonresistance, but there is a third side: We fight with spiritual weapons to expand the kingdom of God.

> For though we walk in the flesh, we do not war
> after the flesh: (For the weapons of our warfare *are*
> not carnal, but mighty through God to the pulling
> down of strong holds;) Casting down imaginations,
> and every high thing that exalteth itself against the
> knowledge of God, and bringing into captivity ev-
> ery thought to the obedience of Christ; And hav-
> ing in a readiness to revenge all disobedience, when
> your obedience is fulfilled (II Corinthians 10:3-6).

Let us keep ourselves from the worldly sword in all its man-
ifestations and throw our whole being into this spiritual war!

Chapter 9

The Oath

Seventh. We are agreed as follows concerning the oath: The oath is a confirmation among those who are quarreling or making promises. In the Law it is command-ed to be performed in God's Name, but only in truth, not falsely. Christ, who teaches the perfection of the Law, prohibits all swearing to His [followers], whether true or false,—neither by heaven, nor by the earth, nor by Jeru-salem, nor by our head,—and that for the reason which He shortly thereafter gives, For you are not able to make one hair white or black. So you see it is for this reason that all swearing is forbidden: we cannot fulfill that which we promise when we swear, for we cannot change [even] the very least thing on us.

Now there are some who do not give credence to the simple command of God, but object with this ques-tion: Well now, did not God swear to Abraham by Him-self (since He was God) when He promised him that He would be with him and that He would be his God if he would keep His commandments,—why then should I not also swear when I promise to someone? Answer: Hear what the Scripture says: God, since He wished more abundantly to show unto the heirs the immutability of His counsel, inserted an oath, that by two immutable things (in which it is impossible for God to lie) we might have a strong consolation. Observe the meaning of this Scrip-ture: What God forbids you to do, He has power to do, for everything is possible for Him. God swore an oath to Abraham, says the Scripture, so that He might show that His counsel is immutable. That is, no one can withstand nor thwart His will; therefore He can keep His oath. But we can do nothing, as is said above by Christ, to keep or perform [our oaths]: therefore we shall not swear at all.

Then others further say as follows: It is not forbidden of God to swear in the New Testament, when it is actually commanded in the Old, but it is forbidden only to swear by heaven, earth, Jerusalem and our head. Answer: Hear the Scripture, He who swears by heaven swears by God's throne and by Him who sitteth thereon. Observe: it is forbidden to swear by heaven, which is only the throne of God: how much more is it forbidden [to swear] by God Himself! Ye fools and blind, which is greater, the throne or Him that sitteth thereon?

Further some say, Because evil is now [in the world, and] because man needs God for [the establishment of] the truth, so did the apostles Peter and Paul also swear. Answer: Peter and Paul only testify of that which God promised to Abraham with the oath. They themselves promise nothing, as the example indicates clearly. Testifying and swearing are two different things. For when a person swears he is in the first place promising future things, as Christ was promised to Abraham Whom we a long time afterwards received. But when a person bears testimony he is testifying about the present, whether it is good or evil, as Simeon spoke to Mary about Christ and testified, Behold this (child) is set for the fall and rising of many in Israel, and for a sign which shall be spoken against.

Christ also taught us along the same line when He said, Let your communication be Yea, yea; Nay, nay; for whatsoever is more than these cometh of evil. He says, Your speech or word shall be yea and nay. (However) when

one does not wish to understand, he remains closed to the meaning. Christ is simply Yea and Nay, and all those who seek Him simply will understand His Word. Amen.
—*Schleitheim Confession, Article VII*

Of all the many characteristics of the faithful church through the centuries, nonresistance and non-swearing of oaths are perhaps the most persistent. The Waldensians, the Bohemian Brethren, the Lollards, and the Anabaptists all stood solidly against the swearing of oaths (although the Lollards were not completely clear on nonresistance). No matter what else a particular group did or did not understand, they were nonresistant and non-swearing.

Back in those days, to be against swearing oaths was a serious thing. In ancient and medieval times, society essentially ran on oaths. Nearly every activity required an oath. To decide to stop taking oaths in the Middle Ages would instantly mark one out as a "heretic"—and arrest, torture, and execution could follow. For example, in the Swiss canton of Berne,

> Anabaptists' refusal to swear oaths was the greatest single stumbling block to their acceptance by the Bernese authorities from the early sixteenth to nineteenth centuries. The oath formed the basis of the Bernese legal system, since God was seen as the only guarantor of the truth of a sworn testimony or agreement. Religious differences were minimally important to the government.[63]

Today, to be against swearing oaths is not nearly as serious a matter. If we must testify in court, we simply request to affirm rather than swear, and no one objects.

63   Mark Furner, "On the Trail of Jacob Ammann," *Mennonite Quarterly Review* 74(2) (April 2000):326-328, p. 327.

Nevertheless, we must keep this conviction alive by God's help or it may disappear under pressure.

Oaths Under the Law

Amid the flames, clouds, smoke, and trumpetings on Mount Sinai, God gave a covenant to Moses for the people of Israel. This law would be the standard of righteousness until the Messiah came to replace it. The Mosaic Law has plenty to say about oaths, and it is essential to understand exactly what the Law allowed and did not allow when we are discussing the subject of oaths.

Under the Law of Moses, oaths were permitted, and the children of Israel made extensive use of them in Old Testament times. In fact, under certain circumstances, the Law actually commanded the use of oaths. In Exodus 22:10-12, we read:

> If a man deliver unto his neighbour an ass, or an ox, or a sheep, or any beast, to keep; and it die, or be hurt, or driven away, no man seeing *it*: *Then* shall an oath of the LORD be between them both, that he hath not put his hand unto his neighbour's goods; and the owner of it shall accept *thereof,* and he shall not make *it* good. And if it be stolen from him, he shall make restitution unto the owner thereof.

In the book of Deuteronomy, God includes swearing by His Name as part of the service which He desired from the Israelites and mentions it in the context of a rejection of idolatry.

> Thou shalt fear the LORD thy God, and serve him, and shalt swear by his name. Ye shall not go after other gods, of the gods of the people which *are* round about you; (For the LORD thy God *is* a jealous God among you) lest the anger of the

LORD thy God be kindled against thee, and destroy thee from off the face of the earth (Deuteronomy 6:13-15).

Thou shalt fear the LORD thy God; him shalt thou
serve, and to him shalt thou cleave, and swear by
his name. He *is* thy praise, and he *is* thy God, that
hath done for thee these great and terrible things,
which thine eyes have seen (Deuteronomy 10:20-
21).

Oaths were also required in the service of the priests.
Numbers 5:11-31 records what was to be done with a woman who was suspected by her husband of unfaithfulness. She
was to be brought to the priest, who was to perform a ceremony to allow the Lord to reveal whether she was guilty or
innocent. Part of this ceremony involved an oath.

So we see that not only were oaths permitted under the
Law of Moses, they were actually required in some circumstances. Nevertheless, there were restrictions which were
applied even under the Mosaic Law which are important to
understand.

If a man swore to do something and was unable to perform it, the Law considered it sin and required that he bring
a trespass offering to the priest (Leviticus 5:4-6; see also
Numbers 30:1-2). Swearing falsely was also forbidden (Leviticus 6:2-5; 19:12; Zechariah 8:16-17; Malachi 3:5). Near
the end of his life, Joshua warned against swearing by the
names of false gods (Joshua 23:6-8).

Oaths were not a light thing among the ancient Israelites. They took oaths very seriously. An example of this is
found in Joshua 9. Having been fooled into thinking that the
Gibeonite representatives had come a long distance from
their homeland, Joshua "made peace with them, and made a
league with them, to let them live: and the princes of the con-

gregation sware unto them" (verse 15). Making peace with these people was against the Law of God, but when they discovered their error, they had to keep peace with these heathen for the sake of the oath (verses 18-21). Centuries later, the house of King Saul was judged because he had broken this oath (II Samuel 21:1-9).

So we see that with some important exceptions, oaths were permitted and even required under the Old Covenant. But the day came when the reign of the Law of Moses ended.

A New Kingdom

"Repent ye: for the kingdom of heaven is at hand," cried John the Baptist (Matthew 3:2). People from all over Judaea flocked to hear this man, dressed in camel's hair, preach about the coming of the new kingdom. Then one day, John greeted the King Himself with these words: "Behold the Lamb of God, which taketh away the sin of the world" (John 1:29b). "The law and the prophets *were* until John," Jesus later said; "since that time the kingdom of God is preached, and every man presseth into it" (Luke 16:16). The reign of Moses' Law had ended, and the King was here to establish the laws by which His kingdom would operate. Among the laws which He set up was a radically different standard on the swearing of oaths.

Jesus' Words on Oaths

Jesus addressed the subject of oaths in the most influential sermon of all time, the Sermon on the Mount. In Matthew 5:33-37, we read:

> Again, ye have heard that it hath been said by them of old time, Thou shalt not forswear thyself, but shalt perform unto the Lord thine oaths: But I say

unto you, Swear not at all; neither by heaven; for it is God's throne: Nor by the earth; for it is his footstool: neither by Jerusalem; for it is the city of the great King. Neither shalt thou swear by thy head, because thou canst not make one hair white or black. But let your communication be, Yea, yea; Nay, nay: for whatsoever is more than these cometh of evil.

Jesus made clear the radical new standard which He was requiring of those in His kingdom – no oaths at all, for any purpose, in any way. "Swear not at all," He said. There is nothing unclear about this instruction.

For centuries, men have tried to obscure and subvert this clear instruction. Many commentators and theologians have said that Jesus only prohibited false and frivolous oaths, not true and necessary ones. It has also been claimed that what Jesus was *really* saying was that it would be better to never swear than to swear hypocritically. Both of these "interpretations" run counter to what Jesus *actually said*: "Swear not at all." If He had meant something else, He would have said so.

James' Words on Swearing

Jesus was not the only one to instruct the citizens of the kingdom of God to abstain from swearing. The Apostle James wrote:

> But above all things, my brethren, swear not, neither by heaven, neither by the earth, neither by any other oath: but let your yea be yea; and *your* nay, nay; lest ye fall into condemnation (James 5:12).

James tells us "swear not," and then instructs us to avoid swearing by heaven, earth, or "by any other oath." "Any other" would include swearing by God Himself.

This verse also gives us the answer to the question "is the subject of swearing really all that important?" The Book of James discusses many topics – responding to the trials of life, partiality, the relationship of faith and works, controlling our tongues, strife, separation from the world, wealth, etc. These are undoubtedly important issues. Nevertheless, when he arrives at the topic of swearing, he begins with "But above all things, my brethren" – in other words, this one topic is more important than anything else discussed in the entire book!

Did Paul Swear?

Some have claimed that Paul swore many oaths in his letters and so it is permissible for us to swear. But what did Paul actually say? Did he ever say "I swear" in his letters?

- "For God is my witness, whom I serve with my spirit in the gospel of his Son, that without ceasing I make mention of you always in my prayers" (Romans 1:9).
- "I say the truth in Christ, I lie not, my conscience also bearing me witness in the Holy Ghost" (Romans 9:1).
- "But *as* God *is* true, our word toward you was not yea and nay" (II Corinthians 1:18).
- "Moreover I call God for a record upon my soul, that to spare you I came not as yet unto Corinth" (II Corinthians 1:23).
- "The God and Father of our Lord Jesus Christ, which is blessed for evermore, knoweth that I lie not" (II Corinthians 11:31).
- "Now the things which I write unto you, behold, before God, I lie not" (Galatians 1:20).
- "For God is my record, how greatly I long after you all in the bowels of Jesus Christ" (Philippians 1:8).

- "For neither at any time used we flattering words, as ye know, nor a cloke of covetousness; God *is* witness" (I Thessalonians 2:5).
- "Whereunto I am ordained a preacher, and an apostle, (I speak the truth in Christ, *and* lie not;) a teacher of the Gentiles in faith and verity" (I Timothy 2:7).

The claim by those who support oaths is that the definition of an oath is calling God to witness to the truth of a statement. If this is the true definition of an oath, then Paul obviously did swear in these verses. But is this the true definition of an oath? Let us look at what Jesus said about the hypocritical oaths of the Pharisees:

> Woe unto you, *ye* blind guides, which say, Whosoever shall swear by the temple, it is nothing; but whosoever shall swear by the gold of the temple, he is a debtor! *Ye* fools and blind: for whether is greater, the gold, or the temple that sanctifieth the gold? And, Whosoever shall swear by the altar, it is nothing; but whosoever sweareth by the gift that is upon it, he is guilty. *Ye* fools and blind: for whether *is* greater, the gift, or the altar that sanctifieth the gift? Whoso therefore shall swear by the altar, sweareth by it, and by all things thereon. And whoso shall swear by the temple, sweareth by it, and by him that dwelleth therein. And he that shall swear by heaven, sweareth by the throne of God, and by him that sitteth thereon (Matthew 23:16-22).

Here we see Jesus rebuking the Pharisees for their rules concerning which oaths could be broken without guilt and which ones had to be kept inviolable. Notice what these oaths were made by: the temple, the gold of the temple, the altar, and the gift on the altar. Although these were oaths and Jesus treated them as such, none of them were "calling God to witness"!

We see then that this is not the true definition of an oath. A true, complete oath has two parts: 1) the actual oath ("I swear") and 2) the confirmation: what is being sworn by. In the verses quoted above, Paul did not swear oaths. He called on God to confirm his words, or affirmed the truth of them himself, but he did not swear.

Application for Today

To take a stand against swearing oaths is, at first glance, not nearly as costly a decision today as it was for the early Anabaptists. They decided to stand with Christ on this issue at risk of life and limb. Today, if we want to take a stand against oath-swearing, we simply ask to affirm instead of swear if necessary, and no one seems to care. Nevertheless, Jesus' teachings about oaths ought to affect our lives profoundly.

Jesus wants our yes to be yes and our no to be no. James says the same thing. Our speech ought to be so reliable that we do not need oaths to confirm it. We should be known as honest people because Jesus has transformed our lives. We do not need oaths anymore because everyone knows that whatever we say will be true and reliable.

We also must be careful in our everyday speech to avoid oaths. Interjecting "I swear" into a conversation is an oath, a violation of the command of Jesus Christ. Such expressions as "by George," "by Jove," or even "by golly" are abbreviated oaths – the confirmation without the statement "I swear." If we use these expressions, no one will take us seriously when we say we do not believe in swearing oaths. Furthermore, they are, in and of themselves, violations of Jesus' commandments and therefore sin.

Lying and exaggeration must be completely eradicated from our speech. Otherwise, we open ourselves up to the criticism that we refuse to swear because we know we are not telling the truth. May such things never be heard. Rather, may all know that we refuse to swear oaths because we have entered the kingdom of God, with its high standard of honesty, and are following the commands and teachings of Christ and the Apostles which forbid oaths – and everything we say is scrupulously honest and, as God grants power, within the standards of righteousness which He has set for His kingdom.

May we earnestly pray to God that He would tame our tongues. "But the tongue can no man tame; *it is* an unruly evil, full of deadly poison" (James 3:8). God can tame it for us, and a tamed tongue must be one of the most remarkable proofs of a regenerated life. "Out of the abundance of the heart the mouth speaketh" (Matthew 12:34).

The Anabaptists and the Oath

The Swiss Brethren, Dutch Mennonites, and Hutterites all rejected the swearing of oaths as against the commands of Christ and the Apostles. Menno Simons wrote:

> That these things are so your unscriptural glosses [comments, explanations] concerning the oath make plain. . . . you, Micron [a Protestant theologian], say that nothing but light-minded, false oaths are hereby prohibited [by Christ's words on oaths], as if Moses allowed Israel to swear light-mindedly and falsely, and that Christ under the New Testament merely forbade these, notwithstanding that all intelligent readers know that it was not merely allowed Israel to swear truly but it was also commanded them to do so. Lev. 19:12; Deut. 10:20.
>
> If the Israelites then, as you hold, had the liberty in this matter that we have, and if it be such a glorious thing and an honor to God rightly to swear by the

name of God, as you make bold to lie against your God, then tell me (Dear me) why Wisdom did not say, You have heard that it hath been said to them of old, Thou shalt not forswear thyself, and I say the same thing. Instead Christ says, Moses commanded not to forswear thyself, but I say unto you, Thou shalt not swear at all.[64]

Peter Riedemann wrote:

Therefore Christ, in order to drive away the shadows that the light of truth—which light he is himself—may shine upon us, cometh and saith, "Ye have heard that it hath been said to them of old: Thou shalt swear no false oath but shalt perform thine oath unto God. But I say unto you that ye swear not at all. . . .Now, if one should say, as they all interpret it, false and superficial swearing is forbidden, but when one sweareth out of love, necessity and the profit of one's neighbour, it is well done and not wrong—this happeneth when human reason goeth before the knowledge of God, and where human cleverness desireth to rule over the Spirit of God, and not allow itself to be controlled by the same. . . .For truly here one cannot let reason rule or twist the scriptures in accordance with human presumption or opinion, for that is futile, but one must give God the honour and leave his command unaltered. . . .Therefore saith James, "Above all things, dear brothers, swear not. . .lest ye fall into hypocrisy." Here James will have no oath at all, whether small or great, to avoid hypocrisy. Therefore, let men twist it as they will and dress it

---

64   Menno Simons (Dutch Mennonite), *Epistle to Martin Micron*, 1554; translation from J. C. Wenger, editor, *The Complete Writings of Menno Simons*, Herald Press, 1984, pp. 922-923.

up and adorn it as they may, no good will be found in human swearing, for Christ himself saith, "Let your speech be, Yea, yea; Nay, nay: for whatsoever is more than these cometh of evil." The evil one, however, is the devil, that teareth good from the heart of men and planteth evil.

Therefore the devout will walk in the truth, allow it to rule and guide them and hold to the same; whatsoever it stirreth, speaketh and doeth within them, believe and observe the same; and this for the sake of the truth which is God himself, which dwelleth in them. Therefore they neither need nor desire any oath.[65]

The Dortrecht Confession (also known as the 18 Articles of Faith), written by the Dutch Mennonites in 1632, states in Article 15:

Concerning the Swearing of Oaths we believe and confess, that the Lord Christ has set aside and forbidden, the same to His disciples, that they should not swear at all, but that yea should be yea, and nay, nay; from which we understand that all oaths, high and low, are forbidden, and that instead of them we are to confirm all our promises and obligations, yea, all our declarations and testimonies of any matter, only with our word yea, in that which is yea, and with nay, in that which is nay; yet, that we must always, in all matters, and with everyone, adhere to, keep, follow, and fulfill the same, as though we had confirmed it with a solemn oath. And if we do this, we trust that no one, not even the Magistracy itself, will have just reason, to lay a greater burden

---

65   Peter Riedemann (Hutterite), *Hutterite Confession of Faith*, 1545; translation from *Confession of Faith*, Plough Publishing, 1970, pp. 197-198, 204-205.

on our mind and conscience. Matt. 5:34, 35; James 5:12; II Cor. 1:17.[66]

Summary

Let us hold fast to Jesus' words about swearing in these times when our conviction on this subject is barely being tested. Let us also hold fast to His standard of absolute honesty and purity of speech under all circumstances—an ideal which we can allow to challenge us every day of our lives.

---

66   Dutch Mennonites, "Dortrecht Confession of Faith," 1632; translation from *Martyrs Mirror*, Herald Press, 1938, p. 43.

Chapter 10

Postscript

Dear brethren and sisters in the Lord: These are the articles of certain brethren who had heretofore been in error and who had failed to agree in the true understanding, so that many weaker consciences were perplexed, causing the Name of God to be greatly slandered. Therefore there has been a great need for us to become of one mind in the Lord, which has come to pass. To God be praise and glory!

Now since you have so well understood the will of God which has been made known by us, it will be necessary for you to achieve perseveringly, without interruption, the known will of God. For you know well what the servant who sinned knowingly heard as his recompense.

Everything which you have unwittingly done and confessed as evil doing is forgiven you through the believing prayer which is offered by us in our meeting for all our shortcomings and guilt. [This state is yours] through the gracious forgiveness of God and through the blood of Jesus Christ. Amen.

Keep watch on all who do not walk according to the simplicity of the divine truth which is stated in this letter from [the decisions of] our meeting, so that everyone among us will be governed by the rule of the ban and henceforth the entry of false brethren and sisters among us may be prevented.

Eliminate from you that which is evil and the Lord will be your God and you will be His sons and daughters.

Dear brethren, keep in mind what Paul admonishes Timothy when he says, The grace of God that bringeth salvation hath appeared to all men, teaching us that, denying ungodliness and worldly lusts, we should live soberly, righteously, and godly, in this present world; looking for that blessed hope, and the glorious appearing of the great God and our Saviour Jesus Christ; Who gave Himself for us, that He might redeem us from all iniquity, and purify unto Himself a people of His own, zealous of good works. Think on this and exercise yourselves therein and the God of peace will be with you.

May the Name of God be hallowed eternally and highly praised, Amen. May the Lord give you His peace, Amen.

The Acts of Schleitheim on the Border [Canton Schaffhausen, Switzerland], on Matthias' [Day] [February 24], Anno MDXXVII [1527].

—Schleitheim Confession, Postscript

We have now completed our journey of investigating in the light of the Scriptures the issues which were important to Michael Sattler and the other early Anabaptists gathered at Schleitheim. It is definitely encouraging to look at church history and see the various people and groups who have stood courageously for truth no matter what the cost.

However, when we study church history, we must not let our thoughts be turned to wishing we could go back in time to be part of some other group, like the early Anabaptists. We cannot go back in time. The early Anabaptists have run their course and finished their race—their time in building the kingdom of God is up. Now it is our turn. Rather than vainly wishing our outward circumstances (time and place we live) were different, we can rejoice that God has put us where we are for a reason and we can build His kingdom like the early Anabaptists did!

> Who knoweth whether thou art come to the king-
> dom for *such* a time as this? (Esther 4:14c).

Let us pick up the Bible, study it carefully (especially the New Testament), and obey it zealously in the power of Christ. This is walking in the resurrection. Let us then recruit many more members for the kingdom of God. Then, in eternity, we will with the early Anabaptists worship the Lamb Who was slain and is risen forevermore, sitting at the right hand of the Father.

Appendix A

The New Birth

In this book, we have discussed many of the outworkings of a new-born life. All is in vain (if not impossible), however, if the new birth is not present. In this appendix, we will examine what the new birth is.

he great call of the Anabaptist missionaries was "Come and join the kingdom of God!" Are you a member of the kingdom of God? Today, "Examine yourselves, whether ye be in the faith; prove your own selves" (II Corinthians 13:5a). Revelation 21:27 says:

> And there shall in no wise enter into it [New Jerusalem] any thing that defileth, neither *whatsoever* worketh abomination, or *maketh* a lie: but they which are written in the Lamb's book of life.

The ultimate standard of Judgment is Jesus' Words. On Judgment Day, every person will be judged by how his actions compared with the words which Jesus spoke. Jesus said:

> He that rejecteth me, and receiveth not my words, hath one that judgeth him: the word that I have spoken, the same shall judge him in the last day (John 12:48).

We need to take these words seriously!

So two facts stand out: Nothing that defiles will enter the New Jerusalem, and we will be judged by Jesus' words.

Does it not make sense, then, to learn how Jesus defines *defilement*? Let us read Mark 7:20-23:

> That which cometh out of the man, that defileth the man. For from within, out of the heart of men, proceed evil thoughts, adulteries, fornications, murders, Thefts, covetousness, wickedness, deceit, lasciviousness, an evil eye, blasphemy, pride, foolishness. All these evil things come from within, and defile the man (Mark 7:20-23).

Let us take a closer look at some of these. Test yourself as we go along—am I living in defilement or victory?

1. Evil thoughts. The Greek word for "evil" is κακὸς (käkŏs). It is defined as "worthless, depraved, injurious."

2. Adulteries, fornications. Hebrews 13:4 says, "Marriage *is* honourable in all, and the bed undefiled: but whoremongers and adulterers God will judge." Jesus said, "whosoever looketh on a woman to lust after her hath committed adultery with her already in his heart" (Matthew 5:28).

3. Murders. Murder is more than killing someone. The Apostle John wrote, "Whosoever hateth his brother is a murderer: and ye know that no murderer hath eternal life abiding in him" (I John 3:15). If you hate someone, God considers you as that person's murderer! "But I have a good reason to hate him!" you may be thinking. Jesus said, "But I say unto you which hear, Love your enemies, do good to them which hate you, Bless them that curse you, and pray for them which despitefully use you" (Luke 6:27-28). We have no excuse.

4. Covetousness. Covetousness is putting *things* first in one's life, either through greed, desiring unlawful things, desiring someone else's things, or extortion to get things. Colossians 3:5 calls covetousness idolatry. Ephesians 5:3 says that covetousness is not to be once named among the saints.

5. Deceit. Have you ever told a 'white' lie? It was deceit! Any attempt to deceive falls under this category. Revelation 21:8 says that "all liars, shall have their part in the lake which burneth with fire and brimstone: which is the second death."

6. Evil eye. Have you ever looked at someone or something with evil desires or intent?

7. Blasphemy. Have you ever spoken against or thought evil about God?

8. Pride. Every human has been guilty of pride.

Jesus calls these "evil things" which come from the heart and defile the man. Many people think that because we do these things and others, we are sinners. Actually, we are sinners not because of what we *do*, but because of what we *are*, which is manifested by what we do. Jesus reveals that the human heart is the *source* of the defilement, thus the unregenerate man cannot enter heaven – "there shall in no wise enter into it any thing that defileth"!

The natural man has some serious needs. His heart is by nature a defiler and he is defiled by sin. He must be forgiven for his past sins, cleansed from the present defilement of sin, and somehow get a new heart so he can stop being defiled!

Jesus can meet these needs for us!

Jesus can forgive our past sins!

> For thou, Lord, art good, and ready to forgive; and plenteous in mercy unto all them that call upon thee (Psalm 86:5).
>
> Wherefore I say unto you, All manner of sin and blasphemy shall be forgiven unto men: but the blasphemy against the Holy Ghost shall not be forgiven unto men (Matthew 12:31).
>
> And be ye kind one to another, tenderhearted, forgiving one another, even as God for Christ's sake hath forgiven you (Ephesians 4:32).
>
> And you, being dead in your sins and the uncircumcision of your flesh, hath he quickened together with him [Jesus Christ], having forgiven you all trespasses (Colossians 2:13).
>
> I write unto you, little children, because your sins are forgiven you for his [Jesus'] name's sake (I John 2:12).

Our past record of sin can be stricken out and forgiven!

Jesus can cleanse from the defilement of sin!

The prophet Zechariah prophesied of the glorious New Covenant: "In that day there shall be a fountain opened to the house of David and to the inhabitants of Jerusalem for sin and for uncleanness" (Zechariah 13:1).

The Apostle John recorded the prophecy's fulfillment: "But if we walk in the light, as he is in the light, we have fellowship one with another, and the blood of Jesus Christ his Son cleanseth us from all sin. If we say that we have no sin, we deceive ourselves, and the truth is not in us. If we confess our sins, he is faithful and just to forgive us *our* sins, and to cleanse us from all unrighteousness" (I John 1:7-9).

In another place, John wrote: "Unto him that loved us, and washed us from our sins in his own blood" (Revelation 1:5b).

Jesus can give a new heart which will not defile with sin!

God said through the prophet Ezekiel: "I will give them one heart, and I will put a new spirit within you; and I will take the stony heart out of their flesh, and will give them an heart of flesh: That they may walk in my statutes, and keep mine ordinances, and do them: and they shall be my people, and I will be their God" (Ezekiel 11:19-20).

The Apostle Paul testified, "I am crucified with Christ: nevertheless I live; yet not I, but Christ liveth in me: and the life which I now live in the flesh I live by the faith of the Son of God, who loved me, and gave himself for me" (Galatians 2:20).

Paul also wrote, "Therefore if any man *be* in Christ, *he is* a new creature: old things are passed away; behold, all things are become new" (II Corinthians 5:17).

Peter told us that we have been given "exceeding great and precious promises: that by these ye might be partakers of the divine nature, having escaped the corruption that is in the world through lust" (II Peter 1:4). This verse reveals that the promised New Heart is nothing less than God's own heart and nature imparted to us! This is how Paul could say that he is not alive anymore, but Christ lives in him!

How Can We Have These Things?

After reading these marvelous promises, if you have not been made a partaker of the divine nature, perhaps you are longing to have what God has promised to give. Perhaps you are wondering how you can have these gifts. Rejoice, my friend! God has not left us in the dark! He has clearly shown the way in which He wants us to receive His gifts. He will not turn away those who earnestly desire what He has to offer.

Believe

Paul wrote, "That if thou shalt confess with thy mouth the Lord Jesus, and shalt believe in thine heart that God hath raised him from the dead, thou shalt be saved" (Romans 10:9). God will not save someone who does not believe that God has done and will do what He said he has done and will do! Another Scripture says, "But without faith *it is* impossible to please *him*: for he that cometh to God must believe that he is, and *that* he is a rewarder of them that diligently seek him" (Hebrews 11:6).

Repent

Those who seek salvation must also repent of their sins. Peter said, "Repent ye therefore, and be converted, that your sins may be blotted out" (Acts 3:19a). The word "repent" means to think differently, followed by a change in the course of action. In this case, it means "to think differently about sin." This thinking differently about sin—going from loving and living in sin to hating, despising, loathing, and mourning over sin—results in my earnestly asking God to strengthen me to live a new life in victory over defiling sin.

Obey

Jesus did not beat around the bush regarding obedience: "If ye love me, keep my commandments" (John 14:15). Those who love Jesus will obey Him! The Apostle Paul said that he preached "that they should repent and turn to God, and do works meet [suitable] for repentance" (Acts 26:20).

Scripture shows that the new Christian should make receiving baptism his first act of obedience to Jesus Christ. We read in the book of Acts, "Then Peter said unto them, Repent, and be baptized every one of you in the name of Jesus Christ for the remission of sins, and ye shall receive the gift of the Holy Ghost" (Acts 2:38).

This process and plan, whereby God gives a person a new heart, is what is meant by the phrase the NEW BIRTH! The old person is gone, all things are become new! Praise God! The new birth is a radical change of the heart, accomplished only by the Spirit of God, imparting to a person a new mind, new desires, and a new heart. It is marked by a passing away of the old ways and desires. The man now despises and hates sin and with the Holy Spirit's help fights it until it is vanquished in him.

Perhaps this all sounds rather scary to you instead of exciting. Perhaps you realize what this is going to cost you. My friend, being born again will cost you your sin. But this is not something bad! Sin has its pleasures for a little while, but it leads to death. From God's perspective (and the perspective of the newly born Christian), Jesus' turning us away from our sins is seen as the highest and chief of blessings! Peter said, "Unto you first God, having raised up his Son Jesus, sent him to bless you, in turning away every one of you from his iniquities" (Acts 3:26). Paul tells us that "the goodness of God leadeth thee to repentance" (Romans 2:4b).

Turn to Christ Today!

My friend, if you have not experienced the new birth, if you are not walking in victory over sin, please turn to Christ today! Jesus said, "him that cometh to me I will in no wise cast out" (John 6:37b). Paul said "the gift of God *is* eternal life through Jesus Christ our Lord" (Romans 6:23b).

However, if you are living in victory over the sin in your life by the power of God but cannot point to some kind of wonderful experience where you received the new birth, do not worry! The kingdom of God does not consist in emotional experiences, but in power (I Corinthians 4:20). If you have God's power in your life in vanquishing sin and following Christ, do not try to find some wonderful experience. Walk in the victory you are experiencing and praise God!

If you have now accepted the new birth, I would highly encourage you to 1) receive believer's baptism and 2) find a Scriptural church which teaches the whole counsel of God and does not shy away from practicing the "hard" commands of Jesus and the Apostles. Share your new-found faith with others to expand the kingdom of God, and please write to me to share your testimony! May God bless you in your new walk with Him.

Anabaptist Teaching on the New Birth

George Blaurock wrote:

> He lets His Word now point out that man shall be transformed, believe the Word and be baptized, and follow His teachings. Now take heed, oh child of man, turn away from your sins! Be not wicked, ungodly, and blind, while the Physician may be found. . . .God, Your mercy is great to those who

repent, setting them free of all their sins through Christ our Lord.[67]

Menno Simons wrote:

To have a fuller account of resurrection and regeneration, we must bear in mind that all creatures bring forth after their kind, and every creature partakes of the properties, propensities, and dispositions of that which brought it forth. As Christ says, That which is born of flesh is flesh, and cannot see eternal life; and, that which is born of Spirit is spirit, life and peace, which is eternal life. That which is born of flesh, out of earth through corruptible seed, is carnally minded, earthly and speaks of earthly things, and is desirous after earthly and perishable things. All its thoughts, feelings, and desires are directed toward earthly, temporal, or visible things, such things as those of which it is born or begotten. That which is born of flesh and blood is flesh and blood, and is carnally minded, because the carnal mind is enmity against God, for it is not subject to the law of God, neither indeed can it be. Therefore, those who are carnal cannot please God. For they are altogether deaf, blind, and ignorant in divine things. A carnal man cannot comprehend divine things, for his nature is not thus, but to the contrary his mind is adverse and hostile to God. A carnal man cannot understand spiritual things, for he is by nature a child of the devil and not spiritually minded. Hence he comprehends nothing spiritual, for by nature he is hostile and a stranger to God; has nothing of the divine nature dwelling in him, has nothing in common with God,

67   George Blaurock (Swiss Brethren), *Ausbund* #5, c. 1528; translation from *Songs of the Ausbund Vol. 1*, Ohio Amish Library, 1998-2010, pp. 51-52.

but is much rather possessed of a contrary nature, namely, is unmerciful, unjust, unclean, quarrelsome, contrary, disobedient, without understanding, and irreverent.[68]

Michael Schneider wrote:

If you want to be saved, you need to leave sin, follow Christ the Lord, and live according to his will. Christ Jesus came to the earth to teach men the right way to go, to teach them to turn from sin and to follow him. He said: "I am the way the truth and the life, no-one comes to the father except through me.". . . .Those whose sins have been forgiven should live no longer in sin. This is what Jesus Christ, our Lord, teaches us. Those who fall back into sin break their covenant with God. Even greater pain and suffering will be theirs—and their loss will be forever.[69]

Menno Simons wrote:

The regenerate, therefore, lead a penitent and new life, for they are renewed in Christ and have received a new heart and spirit. Once they were earthly-minded, now heavenly; once they were carnal, now spiritual; once they were unrighteous, now righteous; once they were evil, now good, and they live no longer after the old corrupted nature of the first earthly Adam, but after the new upright nature of the new and heavenly Adam, Christ Jesus, even as Paul says: Nevertheless, I live; yet not I, but Christ liveth in me. Their poor, weak life they daily

---

68   Menno Simons (Dutch Mennonite), *The Spiritual Resurrection*, c. 1536; translation from J. C. Wenger, editor, *The Complete Writings of Menno Simons*, Herald Press, 1984, pp. 54-55.

69   Michael Schneider (Philipite), *Ausbund* #82, c. 1536; translation from Peter Hoover, *Secret of the Strength*, 2008, Elmendorf Books, pp. 31-32.

renew more and more, and that after the image of Him who created them. Their minds are like the mind of Christ, they gladly walk as He walked; they crucify and tame their flesh with all its evil lusts.[70]

Peter Riedemann wrote:

This Spirit of Christ which is promised and given to all believers maketh them free from the law or power of sin, and planteth them into Christ, maketh them of his mind, yea, of his character and nature, so that they become one plant and one organism together with him: he the root or stem, we the branches, as he himself saith, "I am the true vine, ye, however, are the branches." Thus we are one substance, matter, essence, yea, one bread and body with him—he the head, but we all members one of the other. Now, because Christ is the root and the vine and we are grafted into him through faith, even as the sap riseth from the root and maketh the branches fruitful, even so the Spirit of Christ riseth from the root, Christ, into the branches or twigs to make them all fruitful. Hence the twigs are of the same character as the root, and bear only corresponding fruit, as Christ himself saith in the parable, "No man gathereth figs from thistles, or grapes from thorns. No good tree can bring forth evil fruit, neither can a corrupt tree bring forth good fruit, but each tree bringeth forth fruit of its own kind." Now since Christ is a good tree and vine, naught but what is good can or may grow, flourish and be fruitful in him.

---

70   Menno Simons (Dutch Mennonite), *The New Birth*, c. 1537; translation from J. C. Wenger, editor, *The Complete Writings of Menno Simons*, Herald Press, 1984, p. 93.

Thus doth man become one with God, and God with him, even as a father with his son, and is gathered and brought into the Church and community of Christ, that he with her might serve and cleave to God in one Spirit, and be the child of the covenant of grace, which is confirmed by Christ.[71]

Jakob Ammann wrote:

Nevertheless, in this way we may surely conform to God's Word and say: If a miser does not turn from his selfishness, and a fornicator from his fornication, and a drunkard from his drunkenness, or other immoralities, [they are] thereby separated from the Kingdom of God, and if he does not improve himself through a pious, penitent life, such a person is no Christian and will not inherit the Kingdom of God. And if he is judged, we are not the ones who judge, rather Scripture judges. Just as Christ says: Whoever denounces me and rejects my teachings, the word that I have spoken has already judged him and will judge him on the last Day. For we know well that God saves no one apart from His Word, for it is truth and there is no lie in it. Where there is no faith, no new birth or rebirth, no penance and improvement, over these Christ has already passed judgment, for He says: If you do not believe that I am the One, then you will die in your sins. And even if there were a person whose life was without fault and he would say to himself: I can indeed believe in my heart, therefore I do not need to leave my wife and children and abandon my property, then surely the reason would be—as

71   Peter Riedemann (Hutterite), *Hutterite Confession of Faith*, 1545; translation from *Confession of Faith*, Plough Publishing, 1970, p. 62.

we can indeed believe—that they will not be persecuted with the cross of Christ and prefer the rewards of humans to those of God.[72]

An Anabaptist Testimony of Salvation

Several years ago I worked in Rapperswil in an inn as a servant. In the inn I saw and heard nothing but gluttony, drunkenness, cursing, and swearing, as well as all kinds of sin and vice. And when I went to church, I heard nothing more than damnation for the Protestant religion, and that no one would be saved in that church. Many a pair of shoes [as it was said] have lasted longer than our faith would. After that I moved to Bubikon where I worked for the country squire Meisen. There I also went to church, but heard nothing other than damnation of the mass-priests and that no one would be saved in that church either. Besides that, what was taught from the pulpit was denied with a godless life. I did not know what to believe, what I should do or refrain from doing. I prayed earnestly to God that He should reveal to me what I should do.

Shortly afterwards, it so happened that a brother from Moravia was hired by the squire as a miller. Once when we were together in a room, I complained to him that I could not make heads or tails of what I should believe. He said to me, if in a room five or six different religions were together at a table gorging themselves, drinking excessively, and gambling, then none of the religions would be

---

72   Jakob Ammann (Amish), "Long Letter," 1693; translation from John D. Roth, translator, *Letters of the Amish Division: A Sourcebook*, 2nd edition, Mennonite Historical Society, 2002, pp. 34-35.

the right faith, because it needs works as well, since without works, faith is dead. God does not want hearers of the Word only; he also wants doers of His Word. One must hear the Word of God and keep it if one wants to be saved. Then I called earnestly on God that He would reveal to me where the right faith could be found. Next I came to Zurich and bought this little catechism and read diligently in it.

I prayed further to God and received the Lord's Prayer for myself. Then God revealed to me that when I say 'Our Father,' it means that God is my Father and I am his child. As the Father is holy, so should I as his child also be holy. And when I say 'who art in heaven,' I believe that my fatherland is not here on earth, but in heaven where my Father is. Therefore I should not search for that which is of this world.[73]

---

73   Galli [Fuchs?] (Swiss Brethren), discussion between Reformed officials and Anabaptists, 1613; translation from James Lowry, translator, *Hans Landis*, Ohio Amish Library, 2003, pp. 33, 35. Unfortunately, the secretary chose not to record the rest of what Galli said!

Appendix B

Congregational Order

This document was probably written in 1526, before the Schleitheim Confession. It has been discovered bound with the Schleitheim Confession. It is believed to be the oldest Anabaptist church Order (*Ordnung*). Translation by Peter Hoover; used by permission.

Since the almighty, eternal, and merciful God has made his wonderful light break forth in the world in this most dangerous time, we recognise the mystery of his will. His will is for his Word to be made known to us so we may find our way into community with him. For this reason, and in obedience to Jesus' and the apostles' teaching, we are to observe a new commandment—the commandment to love one another so we may live in brotherly unity and peace. To keep that peace all of us brothers and sisters have agreed as follows:

1. To meet at least three or four times a week, to exercise ourselves in the teaching of Christ and his apostles, to admonish and encourage one another from the heart to remain faithful to Jesus as we have promised.

2. When the brothers and sisters meet, they shall choose a Scripture to read together. The one to whom God has given the best understanding shall explain it, the others should be still

and listen, so that there are not two or three carrying on a private conversation, bothering the others. We shall read from the Psalms every day at home.

3. Let none be careless or act foolishly, either in word or action. Everyone should behave in an orderly way, especially before unbelievers.

4. When a believer sees his brother in the wrong, he shall warn him according to the command of Christ, and admonish him in a Christian and brotherly way, in love.

5. Of all the brothers and sisters of this congregation none shall have anything of his own, but rather, as the Christians in the time of the apostles held all things in common, and stored what they had in a common fund, so they should help the poor, and give to everyone according to his need. As in the apostles' time, none of the believers should be allowed to suffer want.

6. All gluttony shall be avoided among the believers. Serving soup should be enough, or a small amount of vegetables and meat per person, for the Kingdom of Heaven does not consist of eating and drinking.

7. Every time the believers meet for worship, they should break bread and drink wine to proclaim the death of the Lord. Everyone should remember, through this, how Christ gave his life for us, how his blood was poured out for us, so we may become willing to give our bodies and lives to Christ—that is to all our brothers and sisters in him.

Appendix C

References for Anabaptist Material

If you would like to learn more about what the early Anabaptists believed, you can read the following books. Books marked with an asterisk (*) are primary sources (written by the Anabaptists themselves). Most material is limited to the period 1520-1575. These references will tell you what the Anabaptists believed; however, if you would like to know what God believes, read the Bible!

*Songs of the Ausbund. 2 volumes. Ohio Amish Library.

*The Chronicle of the Hutterian Brethren. 2 volumes. Plough Publishing.

Estep, William R. The Anabaptist Story. William B. Eerdmans Publishing Company, 1996.

Friedmann, Robert. The Theology of Anabaptism. Herald Press, 1973.

*Gross, Leonard (editor). Golden Apples in Silver Bowls. Lancaster Mennonite Historical Society, 1999.

Horsch, John. Mennonites in Europe. Rod & Staff Publishers. 1950 (republished 1995).

*Hutter, Jakob. *Brotherly Faithfulness: Epistles from a Time of Persecution*. Plough Publishing, 1979.

*Klaassen, Walter (editor). *Anabaptism in Outline*. Herald Press, 1981.

*Lowry, James W., trans. & ed. *Hans Landis: Swiss Anabaptist Martyr in Seventeenth Century Documents*. Ohio Amish Library, 2003.

*Marpeck, Pilgram. *The Writings of Pilgram Marpeck*. Herald Press, 1978.

*Philips, Dirk. *The Writings of Dirk Philips*. Herald Press, 1992.

*Riedemann, Peter. *Peter Riedemann's Hutterite Confession of Faith*. Herald Press, 1999.

*Riedemann, Peter. *Love is Like Fire*. Plough Publishing, 2011.

*Roth, John D. *Letters of the Amish Division: A Sourcebook*. Mennonite Historical Society, 2002.

*Sattler, Michael, et al. *The Legacy of Michael Sattler*. Herald Press, 1973.

*Simons, Menno. *The Complete Writings of Menno Simons*. Herald Press, 1984.

Ste. Marie, Andrew V. "Early Anabaptist Groups." *The Witness* 10(6) (June 2012):4-14.

*van Braght, Thieleman J. *Martyrs Mirror*. Herald Press, 1938.

Several of these titles are available from *Sermon on the Mount Publishing*.
To contact us, write to:
Sermon on the Mount Publishing
P.O. Box 246
Manchester, MI 48158

Phone: (734) 428-0488.

E-mail: the-witness@sbcglobal.net.
Website: www.kingdomreading.com.

For more excellent titles and other material by the same
author, call or write for a free catalog:

Sermon on the Mount Publishing

P.O. Box 246
Manchester, MI 48158
(734) 428-0488

the-witness@sbcglobal.net

www.kingdomreading.com